MENTAL EXERCISE

FOR DOGS

The 101 best dog games for more agility, intelligence and fun

Sina Eschenweber

1st edition

Sina Eschenweber

1st edition

2020

ISBN : 9798566060880

Table of contents

About the author.. 1

Introduction 3

Why is playing and activity so important for dogs? 7

Playing with dogs for wellness and IQ 12

Exercise and physical activity 15

How to correctly identify the needs of dogs 21

Differences and preferences of different dog breeds..........30

Interpreting the body language of dogs correctly 37

The basic rules for carefree playing 41

Playing with children 45

The right toys 47

The basic commands – essentials for a great play time 50

Outdoor and indoor fun

– the fun factor for every human-dog-team 57

Search games and scent games 58

Hunting games and prey-related games 67

Movement games for more fitness......................................76

Outdoor games – fun in the great outdoors......................104

Indoor games – fun in the house and in the apartment ...135

Food games 166

Diving and water games 184

Intelligence and brain games..193

Balancing games...221

Conclusion..228

Disclaimer 231

Copyright..232

Imprint 233

About the author

Animals have always been the passion of author Sina Eschenweber. In the past, it was first cats she grew up with, and then, at the age of 13, she got her first dog. Today, the author Sina Eschenweber lives together with her boyfriend in a large apartment with a garden and has three dogs: two Labradors and a Berner Sennen. All three dogs came to her when they were puppies, and because of her passion, the author has completed training as an animal keeper and can therefore always use her knowledge when handling and training them.

In addition, the father of her friend is a veterinarian and has therefore, from the beginning, given very helpful tips on nutrition, education and games, and in general how to handle dogs. The author, who otherwise prefers to write about nutrition and health, would now like to pass on her passion and her collected knowledge to her readers. After all, especially when a dog first moves in, there are a few things to consider from the very beginning to ensure that it is properly nourished and educated so that long walks, excursions and trips as well as living together in everyday life are possible. The author loves walking and exercising her three dogs along with spending many hours writing at her computer. Meanwhile, Sina Eschenweber is a full-time author and helps out at the weekends as well as twice during the week at the animal shelter in order to have as much contact as possible with animals.

Introduction

Dogs are very intelligent, and they specifically want to be challenged and encouraged. Nevertheless, every one of our four-legged friends has its own interests, needs and abilities. Occupation is an essential requirement for dogs, but to a large extent the right form of occupation is very important.

The dog is considered man's best friend, and indeed, you will give your furry friend the greatest pleasure if you take enough time for it. Actually, this fact is unique in behavioural biology: there is no other animal species that prefers a human as its social partner over its own conspecifics, but this in no case means that dogs do not need conspecifics. On the contrary, regular contact and playing together are important for optimal development and also for the ability to behave correctly when interacting with other dogs. But without humans, the social development of the dog cannot succeed either. Your four-legged friend needs you and is definitely not only dependent on you in terms of health and nutrition. Its well-being and sociability depend to a large extent on how we humans deal with it, keep it busy and train it to be a cooperative companion in a shared world.

Dogs are by nature designed to move around a lot. The ancestors of our current four-legged friends were busy all day long tracking down prey, following certain tracks, going hunting and killing prey.

This urge to move is still anchored in dogs today – perhaps in some more than others. Most dogs are therefore not satisfied with just going for a walk but make completely different demands on their master or mistress.

It is therefore crucial to ensure that boredom does not arise, but don't worry, there are numerous ways to promote your dog's agility, intelligence and their relatedness to humans. This book aims to show you which dog games are exciting, clever and a real pleasure to play. It allows you to actively involve your dog in many different areas of life, such as daily walks, at home, on vacation and even in the office! There are innumerable possibilities for activities, which will not only give your dog, but certainly also you, a lot of joy. You will get to know a whole range of them in this book.

This book is designed to help you understand the reactions of your four-legged friend better and better. Learn how your dog expresses joy and frustration, when it seems to be overwhelmed and what it finds particularly difficult or easy. Only when you have succeeded in establishing this inner connection will you be able to choose exactly the right thing for your dog from the numerous possibilities for activity.

To be active together is great because playing together means learning together at the same time. Through intensive interaction with the dog, you will be more and more able to interpret its reactions correctly.

In addition, your dog stays healthy and also trains its discipline and endurance! Your dog will become an attentive companion that is always curious and eager to know what you have thought of next for it.

I hope you enjoy reading, discovering and playing with your four-legged friend!

Why is playing and activity so important for dogs?

For us humans, playing is often like a little escape from everyday life, bringing variety and fun into our own lives. For dogs, playing extensively also means joy, the reduction of aggression, and relaxation. But this is about more than just fun. While playing, dogs train their coordination, learn to work better with humans, burn off energy and discover new favourite activities in everyday life.

However, it is crucial that games are played without a stress factor. To occupy your four-legged friend intensively from morning to evening is not the intention. Every dog needs its rest time, just like its master or mistress. Therefore, there should not be any stress when you decide to spend time with your dog. Quite the opposite; rather, experience consciously the togetherness and perceive the needs of your four-legged friend. Try to achieve a balanced mixture between different sources of stimulation and play as well as resting phases. In this way you can consciously train its abilities. The result: you are satisfied and so is your dog!

By the way:

A great activity programme includes more than just playing. It also includes social contact with other dogs, walks, ample opportunity to let off steam and sniff around, and encounters with people. The only important thing is that it matches the temperament of your dog.

When dogs are not busy sleeping or eating, they want to play – especially young dogs. When playing, they conquer the world and develop important techniques for everyday life without stress.

Then your dog learns, for example:

- To improve sensory perception and body control.

- To perfect genetically based abilities such as the hunting instinct.

- To improve its reaction capacity.

- To develop appropriate behaviour towards conspecifics and humans.

- To find its own place in its social environment – thus to fit into a hierarchy.

Especially with young dogs and puppies, nothing really works without playing, but even for adult animals – and even for senior dogs – the fun should not stop. This is very important to keep your pet physically and mentally fit.

No matter whether the lively Jack Russell Terrier, the Dalmatian, the Labrador or the Small Münsterländer, all these breeds have one thing in common: the behaviours and dispositions originally created by targeted breeding are still present in these dogs, and depending on breeding type and breed, in some dogs more than others. It is important to realise that each breed of dog has its own needs and that any form of activity, as well as any type of dog game, should be adapted to the breed, the temperament and the character of the dog. Larger breeds that love hunting, exploring the environment or a large territory need correspondingly more exercise and activity than others. This point should always be considered when choosing a dog breed before buying the dog. Otherwise, it can happen that your dear, sweet Shepherd mix is very dissatisfied quickly because you may only have 30 minutes to spare for a leisurely walk every day. This is really not enough to meet the predisposition and the needs of such a dog breed.

Therefore, before acquiring a dog, think

about the time you have available, about your everyday life, how much space you have and of course about the needs of y-our (future) dog. Every family and every household are different, and it makes no sense if you, as a perhaps very active family or as a very sporty couple, acquire a dog that cannot keep up at all or that, the other way around, needs much more than you can give it in this respect.

You don't have to go hunting with a Hound or sledding with a Husky for your dog to be truly happy. However, do think about possible games that suit it and about how to keep the dog appropriately occupied to prevent later disappointment or sudden stress from the start. Just because you think a breed is beautiful, such as a German Shepherd, a Dalmatian or a Husky, does not automatically mean that it will suit you and your lifestyle.

Playing with dogs for wellness and IQ

Our modern lifestyle often leads to chronic underemployment among our dogs. When playing, however, our four-legged friends can live out their natural behaviour: catching prey (even if it is only a plaything), hunting and tracking.

Do you sometimes curse your everyday life with all its routines and boredom? Your dog has at least as much reason to do so. As humans, we are able to create a distraction for ourselves by, for example, taking a walk through nature, listening to music or reading an interesting book. A dog is not able to get such food for the senses by itself but must dutifully wait until its master or mistress has time for it. But your dog is curious about interesting smells or objects, about grass under its paws or about funny movement games.

Playing together compensates your dog for many a boredom in everyday life, has a stimulating effect and awakens its spirits.

So, your dog can get just as bored as you. You can prevent this boredom by playing exciting games and introducing new tasks and ideas in everyday life. You can also find new routes, which you can explore together. If you want a strong bond between you and your dog, this is also the right approach. The basic premise of this book is that you will find many new ideas for games and a meaningful occupation for your dog so that boredom has no chance. In this way, you will make yourself as well as your dog happy in the long run.

Be guided by the character and temperament of your dog in all games and make sure that your dog is encouraged in a targeted manner. You can only develop your dog's intelligence if you regularly offer it new games and allow it to experience things for itself. Do not predetermine everything for your dog, let it discover, sniff, hunt and explore by itself, in order to provide the necessary exercise at the same time. Even more important than just pure exercise is that your dog can have positive experiences. If you want to have a happy dog and not just a dog that is tired at the end of a walk, then targeted games will help you achieve this. Don't forget to give it a reward at the end of the exercise in the form of praising words or a (favourite) treat. In this way, your dog will be even happier and its bond with you will be strengthened.

Wellness for the dog and the master or mistress can therefore be quite simple, if you just engage in the targeted occupation of your furry friend. In the long run, you will not only strengthen your dog's self-confidence, but also show it that you are reliable and always available. This makes playing with your dog more and more fun over time and it makes everyone happy.

Exercise
and physical activity

Playing promotes intelligence because boredom can dull your dog's senses. A dog suffers when it is kept isolated from its conspecifics or only knows the daily monotony of being taken for a walk, sleeping and eating. This eventually leads to the animal gradually losing its curiosity, its willingness to learn and its social skills. Then whenever encountering anything that the dog cannot classify immediately, it reacts either anxiously or aggressively.

It is therefore of enormous importance to promote the play instinct of the animal purposefully and to offer your four-legged friend new experiences regularly.

Exercise is also indispensable for a dog's health. Don't be fooled by the fact that dogs like to sleep and sometimes seem quite lazy. Every dog, even the smallest breed, needs enough exercise. Your dog can become sick, unhappy and generally dissatisfied if you can't provide it with the necessary amount of exercise.

In particular, because many dog owners do not always have the time for long walks, exciting games and the discovery of new places, many dogs are not fully occupied. In that case, don't make the mistake of giving your dog extra food. Just as with humans, the combination of too little exercise and too much food, particularly in the form of tasty but completely unnecessary snacks, tends to make your dog fat and sick. Even with a job that takes up a lot of time, you should spare a bit of time for your dog, and you must take the time to walk with it at least in the morning and evening.

Give yourself and your dog more exercise and fewer unhealthy snacks. Physical exercise is important for both of you because humans get fatter and more prone to illnesses in the same way when they don't do enough exercise. So go for walks and go jogging or cycling – whatever you want to do, the only thing that matters is that you can take your dog with you. With that much exercise, you'll get faster, stronger and have more stamina – just like your dog!

More agility for your four-legged friend

Would you like to challenge your dog properly and make it more agile? Maybe you remember some obstacle course from your school days or youth, where you had to sprint, jump, climb and run a slalom. This requires the highest concentration, strength and agility and at the same time strengthens your stamina. The same goes for your dog!

If you include a varied training programme with obstacle courses, you can stimulate your dog even more. For example, have your four-legged friend crawl under and jump over obstacles, or set up a course that requires fast running and agility so that it's all about speed and special requirements on the course.

You may even want to join in yourself. Not only is such training a guarantee of more agility, fitness and coordination for dogs, the same applies to us humans!

More than pure exercise: mental work-out required!

When it comes to keeping a dog properly occupied, the focus should not be on exercise alone. Of course, it is very important that you take your dog outdoors and let it play and explore. But that won't be enough if you don't pay equal attention to its mental exercise. For any dog that continues to be restless in your house or apartment after long walks, it may be that your dog has not sufficiently burned off enough physical and mental energy.

In the end, you need to challenge your dog not only physically, but also mentally. Games such as agility training not only stimulate the body, but also the mind and concentration of your dog. Come up with new ways of playing and different games, for example, with the help of this book, so that your dog has to think a little bit for itself. Then things will surely be calmer at home. However, your tasks should not be too special or difficult, otherwise your dog may become discouraged. It should also not use the playful exercises to cause more havoc in your home afterwards simply because it suddenly knows how to lift the funny lid off the box with the pigs' ears, to name just one example. Therefore, don't overdo it and, above all, make sure that your dog is busy without using all the new tricks to bring chaos into your life.

It is certain that walks alone, that is, without further occupation and playful mental effort, are not enough for your four-legged friend. Realise that your dog needs a little more in this regard and respond to these needs as best you can.

How to correctly identify the needs of dogs

Let's take a look at what a dog needs to be happy and relaxed. At the beginning, it can certainly be overwhelming when you realise how many different tasks you as master and mistress have to fulfill. But it looks worse than it is because in addition to sufficient exercise, mental stimulation and a large dose of love, dogs do not need much more to be happy.

There are a few things in a dog's daily life that lead to a happy and fulfilled dog. It takes a little more than good food, long walks and plenty of sleep – but not so much that you would have to worry about not managing these things.

As an example, here is a possible daily routine that will keep your four-legged friend busy, occupied and happy (you should adapt the individual points to your dog's breed and temperament – more details on the needs of the individual breeds can, of course, also be found on the following pages).

1. Exercise in the morning drives away sorrow and laziness!

Start the day with a nice walk, in which short games can be incorporated. This is the perfect way for your dog to start the day and not, for example, lie around lazily in the corner. Morning exercise is really important for your dog, but it doesn't have to be that long: about 45 to 60 minutes are ideal for this.

2. The snack recharges energy reserves

After the walk, your dog needs something to eat and wants to rest afterwards. After all, it doesn't have to be too exhausting.

3. Even more action: the noon hour

Do you not have time for a walk or long play sessions at lunchtime? Then you can use, for example, special toys that are filled with treats that your dog has to work for first. In this way, it is guaranteed not to get bored!

4. Evening workout: sports, fun and games!

Now is the time for a longer workout! Expect to spend a good hour on this part of the day. Alternate between walks with play and training sessions and endurance sports, such as jogging and cycling, so that your dog doesn't get bored. Only after this workout follows the larger food portion of the day, but your dog must first 'earn' it through lots of exercise, fun and playing.

5. Phew, done! How about cuddling on the couch?

The day was exciting, provided your dog with many new experiences and was quite exhausting with so much action. A nice session of cuddling and a large portion of love and attention are now all your dog needs for perfect happiness. Then, most dogs are probably in seventh dog heaven.

The masters and mistresses, who like to be outside in the fresh air and want to make time for their dog, are thus also burning off energy. In total, depending on the breed and the particularities of your dog in terms of character and age, you should expect to spend about two or three hours a day with your dog. For an even more enjoyable and fulfilling dog life, integrate your dog into your daily routine and take it with you on a day trip to the countryside, for example.

Despite the at first seemingly time-consuming occupation with the dog, it is not the case that you have to entertain your four-legged friend around the clock. If you manage to keep your dog busy through exercise, mental stimulation and appropriate games, you don't need to be there for the dog all day. However, before you buy a dog, think carefully about your daily routine, what you have to do every day and how much time you can spend with a dog eventually. Half an hour a day is definitely not enough, no matter what kind of dog it is.

Therefore, think about how you can organise your everyday life. How long would the dog be alone every day? For example, are you at work eight hours a day and you also have a commute of one hour ahead of you and there is no one to spend time with your dog during this period? Then it becomes indeed difficult because in such a case your four-legged friend could feel neglected quite quickly.

Another question regarding the keeping of a dog that should be happy and content is whether there should be other dogs. Without question, it is possible to keep a dog individually and consider it part of the family. You should not personally, however, try to replace other dogs so that contact with them does not simply fall away.

Let's assume that you, your partner or your whole family don't want to take on a second dog. In such a case, you may be able to socialise with other dog owners – and your dog with their dogs – at regular dog training sessions. Or perhaps you have friends or relatives with dogs. There are many ways to organise a kind of 'play date' for your dog.

Contact with other dogs offers numerous benefits and should not be prevented. These benefits include:

• Your dog learns to deal with other dogs in a relaxed manner.

• Dogs can race, play, squabble and interact naturally with other dogs – humans can't replace that.

• Dogs burn off a lot more energy with other dogs than with their owners.

• The right behaviour towards other dogs is learned in this way so that stress when encountering other dogs can be avoided from the beginning.

•   Playing with other dogs helps to keep your dog busy and promotes a happy dog life.

Have you ever wondered if there are situations in which you should intervene when your dog is playing with other dogs? First of all, you shouldn't intervene immediately, but observe calmly. Watch the dogs and check whether there is a good relationship between them, whether the dogs play together in a relaxed manner or whether your furry friend is afraid, becomes restless or is defeated again and again in playful fights. Then it is time to intervene to avoid further difficulties and to show your dog that you are there for it. In this way, dogs become more confident again over time.

Last, but not least, it is helpful to consider where you can meet other dogs and where there are opportunities for them to play with your dog. The following options are generally possible:

- The dog run.

- Dog training with other dogs.

- Meetings with dogs belonging to friends/family.

- Parks/lakes/forests or popular routes for walks.

- Meetings arranged in special groups like on Facebook (at the same time it is possible to take into account a similar age or the same breed).

In all games, make sure your dog is relaxed and stress is avoided. As long as you make sure that your dog is challenged, that it has variety and that you make enough time for it, the satisfaction of your dog will not be long in coming. Please note, however, that the previous points and tips were rather general since every dog has different preferences and dislikes. Furthermore, it should be taken into account that there are different breeds of dogs, which, in turn, have special characteristics, and that is often forgotten. Thus, a herding dog is not to be equated with a hound. Therefore, we will look at the special features of individual popular dog breeds on the next pages before we move on to the varied dog games.

The more aware you are that the breed and character of your dog should fit you and your family, the better it is. This will give you the opportunity to choose a suitable dog and subsequently experience many wonderful years together with a large portion of dog happiness. When choosing your dog, be aware that every breed has a different disposition, which should be considered when playing as well as in any kind of activity.

Differences and preferences of different dog breeds

Every dog is different. That - which also applies to us humans - is to be observed with dogs quite particularly since with the breeding of each variety, certain characteristics are purposefully emphasised. You will soon discover the preferences and characteristics of each breed yourself and should then select the appropriate games that your dog will truly enjoy. Just think of a Hound. You can play any kind of prey-related game with it that involves hunting or tracking down prey. You will soon notice that your dog is happier if you take into account the respective characteristics of its breed. With mixed-breed dogs, this may not be quite so easy, but if one breed becomes more prevalent in your dog, you should deal with the tendencies of that breed accordingly.

To make it easier for you to get started, you will find below a list of the most popular sorts and breeds of dogs and their specific preferences. Of course, there are many other breeds that cannot be mentioned here due to a lack of space, but this overview will help you with a first assessment of the preferences and the corresponding games that are preferred by the individual dog breeds.

Herding dogs: team action

Herding dogs were bred to keep flocks together. Sheep flocks, in particular, are almost inconceivable without herding dogs, and for shepherds it was, and still is, a great relief when these dogs were present on their wanderings. Since the dogs can be guided by certain signals, love to work with humans in a team and need a lot of exercise, they are very happy to participate in all kinds of movement games.

The following dog breeds are counted among the herding dogs:

- Border Collie

- German Shepherd

- Australian Shepherd

- Anatolian Shepherd Dog

- Bobtail

Protection dogs: more security for properties

When it comes to securing properties, protection dogs are without question the first choice. Would you like to have a dog that can protect your house and yard and doesn't quite appreciate teamwork with humans? Then the following breeds are some well-known examples of protection dogs that give burglars less of a chance:

- Rottweiler

- Boxer

- Great Dane

- Schnauzer

- Doberman

Sled dogs: Nordic exercise lovers

Are you looking for a dog that has stamina, can run for a long time and could even pull a dog sled behind it? Then sled dogs are a good option for you because they are characterised by their endurance as well as by their strong urge to exercise and by their independence. The Nordic dog breeds can follow tracks and love movement and scent games, but they are less dependent on the company of humans and less inclined towards teamwork.

The following dog breeds are counted among the sled dogs:

- Husky

- Canadian Eskimo Dog

- European Sled Dog

- Greenland Dog

- Alaskan Malamute

Hounds: the prey counts

There are several breeds specially bred for hunting, which want to sniff out tracks and are always on the hunt for their next prey. Endurance and speed characterise hounds as well as their fine nose. All games that involve a lot of movement, hunting prey or sniffing out tracks are therefore popular with them. Another crucial aspect is that hounds are used to working closely with humans, as this cooperation was, and is, always essential when hunting with hunters.

The hounds include the following breeds:

- Beagle

- Dachshund

- Weimaraner

- Terrier

- Golden Retriever

- Labrador

Companion dogs: together with their human

Humans love the animal companionship of a dog and even in times past didn't need just dogs that could hunt, herd or pull loads. That's why there are the so-called companion dogs, who love to do everything together with their human/humans. Any kind of game is perfect as long as it is done together – so with these dogs you should bring along the desire to play together with your dog and solve exciting tasks.

Here you can find some breeds that belong to the companion dogs category:

- Spaniel

- Poodle

- Pug

- French Bulldog

- Chihuahua

Interpreting the body language of dogs correctly

The dog's body language plays an important role in communication and tells you a lot about the well-being of your four-legged friend. If you want to know whether your dog likes the games and forms of activity, you only need to take a close look at its body language and you can interpret it accordingly. If you are at a loss, it is helpful to seek the assistance of experienced trainers who can tell you more about your dog's well-being.

For example, you can recognise a mood to play very clearly by the look of your dog. An inviting look, a nudge with the nose or a raised paw are often clear signs of this. If your dog's head is then laid to the ground and its buttocks are raised, your dog wants to tell you, 'Let's go, let's play. What are you waiting for?'

Exuberant, cheerful jumping back and forth is also a clear signal for a grand mood to play.

Playing can easily become serious. If you notice that the mood starts to change, you should stop the game immediately. This is the case, for example, when the dog begins to growl. Don't worry, you will be able to tell a 'playing growl' from an angry one. If your four-legged friend starts to bare its teeth, the playing should be over as well. Another alarm signal is when the dog's posture stiffens and the hair on the back of its neck starts to rise. In such a case, the dog ducks, feels threatened and now threatens to attack in turn.

Dogs send out signals – even when playing – which should actually indicate that the playing time is over.

This includes:

- Licking its nose

If your dog does this, it may well be that it has perceived something as a threat or rebuke. Perhaps you have spoken angrily at it? If so, your furry friend just wants you to be nice to it again.

- Turning the head to the side

  Are you perhaps a little too close to your dog? Look away for a little while or take a few steps to the side for a few moments. Wait a moment because the dog usually relaxes again quickly.

- Yawning

  Yawning does not mean that the dog is tired, but that it wants a little peace and quiet. Is the animal possibly experiencing stress?

  Why don't you just give him a little break and see if the yawning subsides again.

- Slowing down and sitting down

  Maybe the game has become too rough for your four-legged friend. If this is the case, you should proceed with the game more slowly and at a more relaxed pace. If you are trying to teach your dog something, you should stop doing so for the time being. Reward your dog for what it has achieved so far and allow him a little rest.

The basic rules for carefree playing

Dogs and humans speak a different language. Nevertheless, it is possible that they can communicate when playing together. To make this a real pleasure for you and your four-legged friend, you should follow a few basic rules.

Become relaxed

First of all, loosen yourself up. When you call your dog to you, you can get on your knees. Talk to your dog with your hands as well. Walk a few steps forward and then stop. The aim is to encourage your dog to run after you. This is already the first hint for your dog to get the message that now is the time for fun and games.

Pay attention to your voice

For the second basic exercise, you focus on your voice. The volume is not decisive, since dogs hear at least twice as well as humans. So, you can reduce the volume a little without any problems. The first prerequisite for using your voice to give commands or express rewards is that you sound friendly. Just like with humans, a good mood is contagious. Practise praising, which is often almost as good as a treat for your dog.

Rewards

You can choose different types of rewards. These can be caresses, praise or treats, but also your dog's favourite toy or game. For your four-legged friend, of course, the treat is the strongest incentive. During the training phase you can reward your dog for every successful step, but reduce this method step by step. It is important that you do not permanently reward your dog with treats to avoid causing it to become overweight. Here, everything should be done with moderation and purpose.

Use frequent praise and stroking as rewards. This pleases your dog, and you don't have to be stingy with that.

The right moment

For the perfect playing experience, it is very important that you are always aware of the following: your dog lives in the here and now. In order for a reward to really work, you should use it at the right moment. Just wait up to one second before you praise your four-legged friend or give it a treat so that your dog keeps the joy of playing and can consolidate what it has learned. However, you should also make sure that you teach your dog the signal for stopping, even while it is still playing.

You are the boss

Even while playing with your dog, you are

the boss. Always be aware of this. This will also give your dog a certain feeling of security, which is good for him as well as for you. You make the rules and decide when to play as well. Besides, you decide what tricks you teach your dog and what rewards you give it.

Playing with children

Dogs and children have a lot in common. They both like to romp around and can get lost in their eagerness to play. This is great on the one hand, but it can also get problematic – especially when fighting or pulling at each other.

When children – whether out of fear or pure joy – start to scream, it is a signal for the dog to get down to business even harder and to take a rougher approach.

If the child simply runs away, this can be a signal for the dog to hunt. This can quickly lead to falls, injuries and abrasions. For this reason, you should keep a wary eye on when the child and the dog play together.

Basically, the golden rule is: not too stormy!

With easy throwing, hide-and-seek or retrieve games, you and the child, as well as the dog in general, are safe.

Children should see from your example how to treat the dog with respect and understanding. In this way, you create the best basis for a strong friendship between animal and human!

The right toys

In general, dog toys should be as firm to the bite as possible and made of harmless materials – such as latex, cowhide, hard rubber, jute or hardwood. Anything that is too small can quickly wander into the mouth and slide down the throat from there. As a result, your dog can dangerously swallow it.

A hedgehog ball, for example, is a very popular toy: it is caught, hidden, retrieved and nibbled. With a hedgehog ball, you will provide your four-legged friend with an excellent activity. However, make sure that the ball is not too small. Do not use balls that are smaller than the size of your dog's mouth, otherwise accidents can occur in the form of swallowing the toy. Large dogs, accordingly, need quite large toys so that no health risk can arise.

A playing rope with a ball is suitable for retrieving and for smaller power and pulling games. Thick ropes are particularly suitable for puppies, for example, because they can train their chewing muscles at the same time.

Various toys are dragged around by our four-legged friends very happily. However, avoid squeaky toys or your dog might forget its bite inhibition against 'squeaky' conspecifics.

The Kong, made of natural rubber, is not only ideal for retrieving and throwing games, when filled with food, it becomes a real activity toy. The Kong is available in different versions and can be filled with various treats, for example, with dog ice cream. The Kong Dental massages the gums of your dog and also helps to remove plaque.

For smaller dogs, the Kong is available in

more plushy materials that make it easier to grab. For dogs with a stronger bite, such as the American Staffordshire Terrier, there are also harder versions. This toy can be used by your dog without your presence and can keep it occupied for hours.

In addition to the toys mentioned, there is a wide range of other toys, such as lick mats, activity dog games, treat balls, snack eggs and sniffing mats and cubes. The latter are especially suitable for puppies as well as for dogs that are not yet really familiar with intelligence toys. The cube can be scented with different scents and thus promotes your four-legged friend's sense of smell. The sniffing cube can be disassembled into its individual parts and hidden. The material is particularly soft so that it can be grasped well, even by small dogs and puppies.

The basic commands – essentials for a great play time

All dogs play, and therefore this play time should be made as interesting and varied as possible.

Strictly speaking, the basic commands are nothing more than tricks: lying down, sitting down or running to another dog are natural behaviours that every four-legged friend shows on its own. Nevertheless, dogs must learn to perform these behaviours based on a human command or signal. In many cases, the execution of these basic commands is the prerequisite for many games and tricks. Therefore, they will be explained briefly in the following.

Command for nudging

This is a popular signal that involves your dog touching something with its nose purposefully. Among other things, this signal is important to create more trust between the dog and its owner because it allows the dog to learn to look directly for support and to nudge the human when it feels unsafe, for example. In this way, you can prevent your dog from running away out of fear or in a situation that does not inspire confidence.

Here's how to train this signal with your dog:

- In the first step, you should hold out your palm to your dog while it stands in front of you.

- Now, you approach the dog with your hand so that the dog, in turn, approaches it. Once this approach occurs, reward the behaviour with a treat.

- The next step is to continue holding out your hand until the dog nudges it with its nose.

- Now, all you need is the appropriate signal word, in this case 'Nudge', so the dog can associate the nudging with the signal. Practise several times until your dog has understood that the signal 'Nudge' in connection with the open hand means nudging this hand.

- Later, you can also teach the dog that it is not only nudging your hand, but also your leg or another part of your body when it comes to this signal.

Command for touching

Here, the dog should touch a certain target or object with its paw.

Especially for problematic dogs, this command is a very valuable aid because it gives the dog sufficient security and reassurance.

- The hand – in the form of a fist – is held out to the dog. The first step is to teach the dog that it is worthwhile to touch the hand with its mouth. Reinforcement again plays a very important role in this context.

- A piece of food is placed in the palm of the hand.

- If your dog now runs to your hand and maybe even sniffs at it with interest, you should reward this behaviour with the treat.

  However, it is important that the dog only sniffs and does not try to get the food out with its teeth.

- As soon as the dog starts sniffing at your hand interestedly, open the palm and give it the treat.

- In the second step, the dog should learn to hold out longer at the hand.

- Now, add the command 'Touch'.

- It is important that your four-legged friend learns to touch only when the command is given to it.

Command for picking up something

With this signal you teach your dog to pick up an object that is on the ground. This signal is combined with a release signal because the trick is that the dog will not drop the object until it receives the appropriate signal. You can ask your dog to pick up objects from the floor or from your hand – combine the demand with the clear signal, 'Pick up'.

You will certainly need a few attempts, but then you can teach your dog that this signal means that objects of all kinds should be picked up or carefully removed from your hand. Reward the behaviour as always so that your four-legged friend knows exactly what to do.

Command for pulling

Imagine this exercise as a kind of tug of war or as if the dog would be pulling against an object. You can develop the command for picking up objects you learned earlier and practise it with a stick or a rope, for example.

The idea is that the dog should pull against the object and not just pick it up from the hand or the ground. Once the command for picking up objects has been implemented and is clear to the dog, you can teach it this new command quite easily.

Outdoor and indoor fun – the fun factor for every human-dog-team

There is no such thing as a 'playing grouch' among our four-legged friends, but as you have already found out at the beginning of this book, there are significant differences in the need for play between the individual dog breeds.

Now, we start with the different kinds of dog games and game ideas – and here you certainly find the right thing for every furry friend!

Search games
and scent games

Dogs have an excellent nose, which far surpasses the nose of any human. The nose is needed to get to the goal in search and scent games. This is something most dogs enjoy, not just hounds with their enormously fine noses, as it is natural for them to use their noses. Some scent games include a prey, others do not, so there is enough variety for dogs of all ages.

1. Tracking search game

Basically, it is quite simple. How about instead of serving the dog's meal in the bowl as usual, setting up a small sniffing buffet?

❖ Just hide some dry dog food in-doors, or outdoors, and let your dog search for its food.

❖ If you first select the hiding places in a closer environment, your dog with its fine nose will immediately notice that there is something tasty to discover and it will set out on its search. It is best to accompany this with a pronounced command, for example, 'Search!'.

❖ If you extend the search area after some time, your dog will know through the command that sniffing pays off!

❖ In order that the scent and search game does not become boring for your dog, you can increase the requirements from time to time.

❖ Not only the 'area of operation' can be increased, also, the terrain can have different degrees of difficulty: in the high grass or between pebbles – be inventive!

**Tip**:

If you play the game more often, your dog will probably try to collect the treats before the game starts. Even dogs like to cheat! You should therefore first distract your four-legged friend or place him in another room.

2. Treasure hunt

Not all dogs are fast thinkers. Thus, start with an easy task. Wrap up a treat in a little kitchen paper and let your dog unwrap it. Once it has understood how it works, you can slowly increase the difficulty level.

❖ Place the wrapped up treat in a small box.

❖ You can later fill it up with crumpled up newspaper to give your dog a bigger task in its search for the 'treasure'.

❖ This game is not only fun, but also enhances your dog's mental development. It has to stretch itself a little to put its head in the box, which is – to top it all – filled with rustling paper. The success in finding a treat there strengthens its self-confidence.

❖ By the way, you do not necessarily

have to hide a treat in the box. Especially for dogs who tend to be a little overweight, it is recommended to hide its favourite toys instead of the treat.

❖ You can also hide several packages in the box. Some have treats wrapped in them, others are empty. This way your dog will have a lot of fun!

3. Treasure hunt under blankets

With this game you particularly train your dog's sense of smell. It is best to play this game indoors.

- ❖ First of all, place several blankets as a pile in the middle of your living room.

- ❖ Hide your four-legged friend's favourite toys and treats under the blankets.

- ❖ Now ask your dog to look for the hidden things.

- ❖ If your furry friend has found one of the hidden objects, it may eat it or play with it.

- ❖ Always hide different things so that it remains really exciting for your dog.

4. Sniffing cube

For this you need a sniffing cube, scents and treats. You will train your dog's dexterity and concentration with this.

- ❖ First, put scent on individual parts of the cube and create a scent track.

- ❖ On the basis of the scent, the dog must now track down the individual parts.

- ❖ Then, put the cube back together and hide it.

- ❖ After that, ask your four-legged friend to look for the cube.

- ❖ If it has found the cube, it will receive a reward.

5. Hide-and-seek with toys

For this game you need dog toys. With it you can strengthen the bond between you and your dog.

- ❖ Take a dog toy and show it to your four-legged friend.

- ❖ Move the toy and encourage your dog to play with some squeaking noises.

- ❖ As soon as your dog focuses on it, hide the toy.

- ❖ Now search for it together with him.

- ❖ Once your dog has finally found it, reward it.

- ❖ Start by showing your dog where you hide the toy. Later, it will have to sniff it out on its own.

6. Outdoor and indoor sniffing fun

In this scent game you can incorporate and try out many variations. Your dog will train its sense of smell, and on top of that it will be glad about the treats.

- ❖ Hide the food chunks in (low) shelves. Place them on chairs or outside on a tree stump or low branch.

- ❖ With ring-shaped food you can also decorate shrubs!

- ❖ Don't miss your dog's stunned face when it discovers for the first time that the hidden food is not on the ground this time.

Hunting games and prey-related games

Since it is quite natural for dogs to hunt prey, i.e. to chase and hunt it, you can integrate various prey-related games into the dog's everyday life. These games, exercise, fun and natural forms of occupation are sure to be quickly met with enthusiasm by your dog.

This area includes, among others, the so-called retrieval games. They combine hunting, obedience and search exercises. The dog reaches its prey, but may not eat it; instead, it must bring it back to its master or mistress. Only then the dog gets its reward. These games promote the impulse control of the dog and also strengthen the bond between dog and human.

Retrieving

When retrieving, dogs learn not only to pick up various objects but also to bring them to their owners. From this basic exercise, many variations can be created when it comes to playing together.

1. Basic game – retrieving

Start with this basic exercise when retrieving. Your dog should be in the 'Place' or 'Sit' position. Now, throw a stuffed animal through the field of vision of your four-legged friend. Make sure that your dog remains in this position until you give it the command. As soon as you give it the appropriate signal, it may begin to fetch the object. If your four-legged friend has done this successfully, reward it with a treat afterwards.

If you are at the beginning of this game, it can be helpful to show your dog the treat once it has the item in its mouth. This will ensure that it comes back to you quickly and you can then give it the treat. Use a word of your choice or a clicker as a command for the starting signal. The clicker is an ideal training tool that sounds similar to a frog clicker at the touch of a finger. With this, you can teach your dog something. For example, a 'click' occurs as soon as the dog performs a certain desired action.

2. Triangle game

It is best to take your dog outside into the garden or into a park. Your dog must first be in the basic position, 'Sit' or 'Place', again.

- ❖ Let your four-legged friend sit down.

- ❖ Now place its preferred toy on the floor a little further away from him.

- ❖ Then, form a triangle consisting of the dog toy, you and your furry friend by taking a few steps to the side or back.

- ❖ Now call your dog to you.

- ❖ It is important that it comes to you first. Then, it should run to the toy and retrieve it.

    As a reward, you can use a treat again.

3. Newspaper deliverer

In this game it is important that your dog gets used to having a newspaper in its mouth.

❖ Start by putting a newspaper roll or some rolled paper in your dog's mouth.

❖ Wait a moment, take it out and reward your four-legged friend: praise it and give it a treat. You should repeat this first basic step several times so that this feeling becomes a habit for your dog.

❖ For the second step of this game you have to think of a command to signal your dog to go and get the newspaper. Take the paper and throw it a few metres away. Your dog should still have it in its field of vision. Now say your command, for example, 'Get the paper'. When your dog then runs off and brings you the newspaper, reward it with a treat.

❖ Repeat this exercise a few times until your dog has internalised it. Next time, throw the newspaper, but go a few steps further away. Your dog should now bring you the newspaper after the command sounds. Again, treats and praise follow as a small incentive for your four-legged friend.

❖ Finally, throw the newspaper where it is usually always left – for example, at the front door. Then, leave the room or hallway and go to the room where you want your dog to bring the newspaper from now on. Say the command for your dog to fetch the newspaper. Repeat this until your dog brings the newspaper to you. Then, it will get another treat as a reward.

4. Retrieving around an obstacle

This game promotes your dog both physically and mentally.

❖ First, prepare an obstacle – for example, a cone.

❖ Now throw the object that you want the dog to retrieve behind the obstacle so that the obstacle is exactly between you and the object.

❖ Then, give the dog the command to retrieve.

❖ When the dog brings the object and walks around the obstacle dutifully, praise it and give it a piece of food as a reward.

❖ You can, for example, use the command 'Run around it' and, if necessary, link it to the command to retrieve.

5. Hunting soap bubbles

For this game you need a soap bubble bottle for children. With this game you will especially promote the coordination of your dog. You can buy soap bubble bottles especially made for dogs in pet stores. For animals with movement restrictions and pain, however, this game is unsuitable.

* Dip the ring into the soap solution and make soap bubbles.

* Show your four-legged friend the soap bubbles that fly through the air.

* Now ask it to catch them.

* Create again and again new bubbles in different sizes and encourage your dog to hunt them.

* Reward your dog if it catches some bubbles.

6. Let's play tag!

❖ Walk a few steps backwards to encourage your four-legged friend to follow you.

❖ Now change direction while running and run back towards your dog, then immediately away from it.

❖ Give it a nudge in between, just like you remember from your childhood. 'Your turn! Now you have to catch me!'

❖ But make sure you give the command 'Enough' before you are both completely out of breath.

Movement games
for more fitness

Movement games are especially fun for dogs. When playing together with other dogs, movement is almost automatically involved because the dogs run, romp around and bring a lot of movement into the game. Dogs want to be able to let off steam and like to put their focus on movement when playing. This works alone, with other dogs or with their beloved humans.

For movement games it is important that you pay attention not only to pure endurance, but also to the mobility of your dog. They promote stamina, improve coordination and help the dog to orientate itself even better to humans.

But be careful as older or sick dogs can have problems with these games, just like puppies. Therefore, they are ideal for healthy and fit dogs that do not have any physical limitations. If you are unsure about your dog, it is best to talk to your veterinarian!

1. Ball on a rope

In almost every pet shop you should be able to buy a hard rubber ball on a sturdy knitted rope.

Time and a suitable playground, such as your garden or a small meadow, are already everything you need for this game with your four-legged friend. With the ball on the rope you can always add a little variety to the walks with your dog.

❖ Let the ball dangle in front of your four-legged friend's nose and let him carry the toy for a while.

❖ Then, say 'Drop it!' and praise your dog. After a while, let your four-legged friend fish for the ball again. If your dog is old or ill, it is important not to hold the ball too high when playing so that it is not encouraged to jump.

❖ Let your dog sit in a meadow from time to time and place the ball on the rope a few centimetres in front of him. Hold the rope in your hand and slowly pull the ball away from your dog. With a little patience you can teach him to sneak up on the prey.

Don't forget the treat as a reward!

2. Let's play ball! – game variations

For these game variations you don't need large equipment, just a few balls, for example, tennis balls.

❖ Let your dog retrieve as usual at first. Then, send the next ball immediately when your dog drops the one it just retrieved.

❖ Your dog will expect you to throw the ball again in the same direction. To bring a little movement into the game, always throw the next ball in

a different direction that is unexpec-
ted for your dog.

❖ How about not just throwing the
ball, but rolling it through a tunnel?
For small dogs, ready-made rustling
tunnels from the pet shop are suitable for this purpose; for larger
dogs you can easily use boxes into
which you cut large openings.

❖ Now and then, you can let the ball
bounce off the ground so that your
dog has to catch it in flight.

❖ In all game variants, however, you
should absolutely insist that your
dog lets go of the ball it just retrieved before you throw the next one.

3. Jumping over obstacles

As long as the age and the health of the dog allow it, jumping games are suitable for every dog. Possible hurdles can be found everywhere outside: narrow ditches or streams, fallen tree trunks, low fences, small walls and hedges, boulders or bales of hay.

❖ Stand with your dog on one side of the obstacle and let him sit in front of it.

❖ Then, move to the other side – initially by crossing the obstacle yourself. Call your dog while walking backwards so that it jumps over the obstacle to get to you. For example, call out 'Jump!'.

❖ Alternatively, you can lure it with a toy or treat. The distance between you, the dog and the obstacle in between can be increased from time to time.

❖ Some dogs find it easier to jump if they can cross the obstacle together with their master or mistress – possibly on a leash first. The dog will then be particularly motivated to do the same as you.

Tip:

It is of great importance to always choose suitable obstacles for your dog and to adapt them to its size and physical abilities.

Also, please do not overdo it with the jumping!

4. Slalom running

First, the slalom parkour for your dog must be set up. In the garden, garden torches or climbing aids from the flower bed are suitable. In bad weather, you can also play with your dog inside. For example, convert larger flower pots or chairs into a parkour.

❖ Set the distances between the individual obstacles relatively large at first so that your dog can get used to running through the parkour.

❖ It is best to hold a food reward in your hand and let your four-legged friend follow your hand slowly.

❖ Two poles or obstacles are perfectly sufficient for the beginning! Take it easy and reward your dog for every small step. Your dog follows your hand up to the first obstacle and gets its first treat there. If it follows you slowly around the first obstacle, it gets its second treat – and so on.

❖ Once your dog has got the hang of it, you can make the parkour more difficult by either narrowing the distances between the obstacles or increasing the speed.

Caution:

For this exercise, slippery tiles or laminate are taboo! The danger of your dog slipping is simply too great. A robust carpet is better suited.

5. Running around obstacles

❖ First of all, provide an obstacle, for example, a filled PET bottle, a cone or similar.

❖ Now place the dog in front of the obstacle and then call it to you.

❖ As soon as your dog has almost reached the obstacle, give it the command, 'Go around!'.

❖ Reward your dog each time it has run around the obstacle.

6. Crawling game

This game promotes your dog's body awareness and also improves its coordination.

You cannot play the crawling game with every dog. Great Danes, for example, are too big for it and would really struggle to crawl with their very long legs.

- ❖ First, estimate the leg length in the bent state as well as the height of your crawling dog.

- ❖ Kneel down and bend one leg.

- ❖ Take a treat in your hand and lure your four-legged friend under your leg.

- ❖ When the dog lies down and begins to crawl, give your command, 'Crawl here!'.

- ❖ Repeat this process several times until your dog understands exactly what to do and you don't need any more treats to lure him underneath your leg.

❖ Finally, you can leave the leg completely off and just give the command to crawl.

7. Jumping over hurdles

This is a physically quite demanding and exhausting game which demands the coordination of your four-legged friend.

- ❖ At first, start with a small obstacle: stack two thick books on top of each other.

- ❖ Now, make another pile of two thick books, which you place a little bit away from the first pile of books.

- ❖ Then, place a bar on top of the two piles and hold it in place for the time being. (The two piles of books are quasi the posts for the obstacle bar.)

- ❖ After that, lure your four-legged friend and encourage it to jump over the bar. Combine the jump with a command, for example, 'Jump!' or 'Hop over!'.

- ❖ Later, place the obstacle higher and

higher, but never exceed the per-formance limit of your dog.

❖ Also, make absolutely sure that it does not jump against the bar and injure itself in any way.

8. High jump

This game is physically demanding, too, but very well suited for training the coordination of your dog.

- ❖ Choose an object that is large enough for your dog to stand on comfortably with all four paws, for example, a low table, a stool or similar.

- ❖ Now, lure it to the object with a treat.

- ❖ It helps some dogs when they can take a run-up.

- ❖ Important: make absolutely sure that the surface of the object – for example, of the stool – is not too slippery.

- ❖ Then, combine each jump with a command such as 'Jump!'.

- ❖ Repeat the process several times.

❖ Gradually increase the difficulty by simply pointing at the object and giving the command to jump from a distance.

9. Rotating around its own axis

Train the coordination of your dog with this game.

❖ Take a treat in your hand and move it sideways past your four-legged friend so that it follows the treat and turns around.

❖ As soon as it begins to turn, give the command, 'Rotate!'.

❖ Practise this step several times until your dog begins to turn, even without treats in front of its nose.

❖ You can increase the difficulty, for example, by adding directional information and teaching your dog to rotate in both directions.

❖ Caution: remember that dogs can also get dizzy.

10. Moving backwards

This game trains the coordination as well as the body perception of your furry friend.

❖ Take a treat in your hand and move it over and behind your dog's head.

❖ Now, give the command, 'Reverse!' and try to encourage the dog to move backwards.

❖ If your dog sits down instead, you can try to move the treat a little backwards under its head, at chest height. However, please do not do this with frightened dogs!

❖ As soon as the dog starts to walk backwards, reward it.

❖ Repeat this process several times until it walks backwards without any treat.

11. Circus tricks

For this game you need a hula hoop, which you can buy for little money in toy shops. For your four-legged friend this is a great piece of sports equipment.

❖ First of all, familiarise your dog with the hula hoop. Let it run through it a few times first.

❖ Next, keep the hula hoop about ten centimetres above the ground. Encourage your pet to jump!

❖ Caution: dogs that are older or have problems with their joints should not jump!

12. Push the ball over

- ❖ Put a ball or something that can be rolled on the floor.

- ❖ Praise your dog when it moves the object with its nose and encourage it with the words, 'Push it over!'.

- ❖ Sit down opposite the dog on the floor and give it supporting hand signals.

- ❖ Praise your four-legged friend for every correct movement.

- ❖ At the end, it gets a treat or an extra-long cuddling and stroking session.

13. Hunting the ball

The further a ball or a stick flies, the more fun a retrieving dog has chasing after it!

- ❖ Always throw the 'prey' away from your dog and never towards him.

- ❖ Even if you want your dog to catch a ball, you should never aim at its muzzle!

    The risk of injury would be much too high in such a case.

- ❖ Encourage your dog to chase after the ball and bring it back to you.

14. Gymnastics for dogs

How about doing gymnastics together with your dog? That goes like this:

- ❖ Sitting: sit on the floor and let the dog climb or jump over your outstretched legs. If you bend your legs, your dog can crawl beneath and through them.

- ❖ Flat on your stomach or on your back: from the prone position, can you get your dog to run around you or climb over you? Alternatively, lie on your back, stretch your legs up and lean them against a wall or a chair.

- ❖ On all fours: get down on all fours and let your dog walk beneath you. If you have a small dog, you might even be able to get it to walk around one of your arms.

- ❖ Standing up: stand with your legs slightly straddled. Can you make your dog march under your legs, circle a single leg or walk a figure eight around both legs?

❖ On a chair: sit on a chair and let your dog walk beneath you, circle one chair leg, go around the whole chair, clockwise and counterclockwise.

❖ With arm action: squat down one arm's length away from a wall and stretch one arm against the wall. Let your dog either pass under your arm or climb or jump over it. Use the other arm to get your dog to make the desired movements. If this works well, you can also try forming your arms into a hoop through which your dog climbs or jumps.

15. Treat toss game

You throw a treat to your dog and it catches it. That would be the dream of many dog owners, but behind it there is often a little bit of practice. In addition, the talents of each dog are differently developed. Respond to your four-legged friend and practise this playfully with it. For your dog this is true brain jogging. It trains its spatial imagination and body coordination and is a lot of fun for dogs and humans.

❖ Prepare a handful of food chunks. Call your dog. Show it the food so it looks at you expectantly.

❖ Pick up a food chunk in your hand. Hold your hand very still. Now, say a word that will announce to your dog in future that food is now approaching, for example, 'Catch!'. Only then will your hand start to move and let a piece of food slide into your dog's muzzle from above. You hand over the food more than you actually throw it. Repeat this procedure at least ten times.

❖ Gradually start to increase the distance between your hand releasing the food and the dog's muzzle. The procedure is always the same: you clearly say 'Catch!' – and only then will your hand start moving and pass the cookie towards the dog's muzzle. Your dog, which wants to get to the food quickly, will try to grab the food by itself.

❖ To find out from which angle and which height your food chunks approach best, practise individually with your dog.

❖ It's important to practise every now and then in between sessions.

16. Walking between the legs

Coordination and attentiveness are required when the dog runs through the leg triangle of its master or mistress at the right time.

- ❖ Start by helping your dog overcome any fears of contact. To do this, first stand with your legs apart, with the dog sitting or standing behind you. Then, lure it with a treat (or a toy) underneath you, between your legs, and praise it a lot when the dog follows your hand with the treat or toy. With a target stick it works like this: you hold the stick first between, then in front of, your straddled legs.

- ❖ The dog is standing behind you. For every touch of the target stick with the muzzle there is a click and treat. Depending on how carefully your dog walks through your legs, close them gradually so that the passage becomes a little narrower each time. The aim is that the dog joins in without showing any signs of fear of contact.

Outdoor games – fun in the great outdoors

1. Tunnel game for dogs

❖ Make it very easy for your dog at first. Cut a large cardboard box so that only a short tunnel remains.

❖ Roll a treat through it and encourage your dog to go through the tunnel.

❖ Of course, you will reward your dog for its courage immediately afterwards. Initially, it's best if your four-legged friend sits in front of the tunnel so that it can look through it anyway.

❖ If your dog does not dare to go through the tunnel right away, encourage it even more.

❖ Reward it for each step in the right direction. A second human game partner, who is familiar with your four-legged friend, can be very helpful. He places himself at the other end of the tunnel where he calls and waves – another encouragement for your dog.

❖ If at first you are not quite sure whether your dog will enjoy playing this tunnel game, just try the cardboard version or turn a sleeping mat with some tape into a tunnel before you buy a dog play tunnel.

Tip:

Do not force your dog through the tunnel by any means – do not push it through and do not pull it to the target with the leash.

2. Dog racing

This game trains both discipline and concentration of your four-legged friend because it has to listen to your signals before it starts running and must not run after the other dogs.

For this game you need at least one other player who also has a dog. The four-legged friends should get along well with each other. Of course, you should have treats in your pocket as a reward.

❖ In this race, it's not the pace that counts at first, but your dog's ability to wait its turn patiently.

The prerequisite for this game is the command, 'Stay!' Your four-legged friend should definitely already be able to do this! In this race, only one of the two (or more) runners is asked to start running.

❖ The other furry friend must remain sitting dutifully at the starting position until the starting signal sounds for it, too.

❖ It is best to practise individually first. During the time spent waiting, your dog is sitting. Then, move away a little, return and reward him for waiting patiently.

❖ Now, train the call. Start with a short distance and give it the command, 'Stay!'.

❖ Then, take a few steps away, stand up frontally to the dog and call it to you in a motivating voice. Praise it joyfully when it comes to you and reward it!

❖ As soon as this works well, the doubles will start. Lead both dogs to the starting point and give them the command to stay.

❖ At the beginning, take only a few steps away and turn around to the dogs. Agree with your game partners who will call their dog to them first.

❖ Ideally, one dog storms towards its owner while the others remain sitting dutifully. Now big praise is due for the dogs!

❖ If the waiting at the start line did not work out, you should lead the early sprinter back to the starting point wordlessly, but in a friendly manner, and start the game all over again.

❖ As soon as the game goes well, you can gradually increase the distances.

❖ As a final round, all dogs may start at the same time! Now, it's all about speed. Who will be the first to arrive? Reward all dogs in any case!

3. Soccer for dogs

For dog soccer you need a big, light ball, for example, a gymnastic ball. If your dog doesn't know this ball yet, you should give it time to sniff at the round 'monster' extensively at the beginning and lose any fear of it. Your four-legged friend should have good basic obedience for this game.

- ❖ Start by rolling the ball towards the goal together with your dog.

- ❖ After a short time, your dog will understand that the ball will move when it pushes it with its nose.

- ❖ Praise it with a treat every time it touches the ball, and it will soon associate the nudge with the nose with something positive.

- ❖ From time to time, extend the distance the ball is to be pushed and finally incorporate curves. At some point, change your position by placing yourself in the goal and encourage your dog to push the ball to you from a certain point.

❖ Once your dog masters the game well, you can, of course, have several soccer-loving dogs play together.

4. Playing frisbee

A prerequisite for dog frisbee is knowing the commands, 'Fetch!' and 'Drop it!'.

❖ There are several ways to play frisbee with your four-legged friend. Freestyle is about showing an individually composed choreography. Another variation is throwing and catching the frisbee in different predetermined long throw zones.

❖ First of all, you should teach your dog some easy exercises – catching on the one hand, and of course retrieving the frisbee to you as quickly as possible, on the other hand.

❖ In the freestyle version, playing frisbee is a little bit like dog dancing. You create a choreography out of different tricks in which you include the frisbee – with or without music. For example, you can let your dog jump through your arms or legs while it is chasing the frisbee, but there are also different throwing techniques for humans, which they can combine for the choreography.

Variant:

Another possibility is to set up a playing field. The further away from you your dog catches the frisbee, the more points it collects.

5. Detective game

Before you hide for this game, you should equip yourself with a reward for your dog – literally, the way to a dog's heart is through its stomach. Of course, your dog will also be happy to be stroked as a reward.

❖ Let your dog wait either in front of the half-closed door or a little further away in the grass. But you might as well wait for an inattentive moment of your four-legged friend and then use it to hide away.

❖ There are many ways to hide: when walking your dog without a leash, just hide behind the nearest bush or tree.

If you want to play the game in your living room, you can hide behind the curtain, the couch or in an alcove.

❖ If you are equipped with a squeaky toy or bone, you can emit a few 'signal sounds' and thus encourage the dog to search for you.

❖ To link the process of searching with a useful command, you can call, 'Search!'. Very important: praise your dog effusively as soon as it has found you.

Tip:

Some dogs need some time to understand that their master or mistress wants to be found. You can make it easier for them to learn that if you go to your hiding place while the dog watches.

6. Tasty treats parkour

First, you need a kind of parkour. At the beginning, it is sufficient to work without obstacles and to place some bigger treats on the route you want to run with your dog. So, in bad weather, you can train in your own living room without any problems.

❖ Let your dog walk along the track beside you to heel.

❖ If it comes dangerously close to a treat, call it to order with, 'No!'.

❖ This game shall protect your four-legged friend. It is of the utmost importance that your dog does not grab everything edible that is in front of its nose. This can save it from rat poison or other sources of danger during a walk.

Tip:

It is best to practise with your dog when it is not very hungry, because that could make the game unnecessarily difficult.

7. Climbing hills

In this game your dog learns to concentrate and to follow your directional instructions independently. First of all, the dog learns to let you send it in a certain direction.

❖ First, choose a hillock and stand in front of it with your dog.

❖ Then, send your dog onto the slope with a movement of your arm and a signal word, for example, 'Up!'.

❖ If the dog only takes one or two steps and then stops the running movement, the slope is too high. In such a case, choose a lower one.

❖ If everything goes as desired, the dog gets praised and a treat on the spot will increase its joy.

❖ Then, call the dog back to you with your usual command – this behaviour will also be rewarded.

❖   Send the dog up the small slope one or two more times. That is enough for now.

❖   As a next step, you can train your four-legged friend to do small exercises on the slope, such as sitting or lying down. Of course, it gets praised a lot for this every time. Then, you call it back again.

8. Touching branches

For this game you need a clicker. At the touch of a finger, it sounds similar to a frog clicker. It is an ideal training tool to teach your four-legged friend something. For example, a 'click' occurs as soon as the dog performs a certain desired action.

With this game, you teach your dog to independently follow a directional instruction and to perform a certain action at the desired place.

❖ With the help of the clicker, you first teach your dog to touch a stick with its nose.

❖ To do this, you stand near to your dog, holding, for example, a branch loosely in your hand and waiting for the dog to sniff at it curiously.

❖ For each sniff of the branch, there is a 'click!' and a treat.

❖ Once the dog has understood what

it's all about, namely touching the branch, you further shape its behaviour with the help of the clicker. Now, the dog should learn to touch the branch only at its end. Click each time the dog touches the branch a little further down (don't forget the treat).

❖ If the dog reliably only touches the end of the branch with its nose, you can now easily direct your four-legged friend everywhere, and with pinpoint accuracy.

9. Tug of war with your four-legged friend

You need a dog rope for this game. With this game you strengthen the bond between you and your dog.

- ❖ Offer your four-legged friend a rope.

- ❖ As soon as your dog holds the rope between its teeth, carefully pull the other end.

- ❖ Let your dog measure its strength for about 30 seconds.

- ❖ Then, end the game with the command, 'Drop it!'.

- ❖ Please do not pull the rope too strongly to avoid damaging the dog's teeth. This applies especially to puppies!

- ❖ Let your dog win and take the rope for itself.

10. Outdoor sniffing fun

This is a special fun game for outside and especially for early risers. It is necessary for your dog to already follow the commands for sitting and lying down.

- ❖ It is best to ask somebody to help you by keeping your dog on a leash.

- ❖ Now, take 10 to 15 steps straight ahead across a lawn, preferably when the grass is still dewy.

- ❖ There, place your dog's favourite toy or a larger piece of food – for example, a treat ball – on the ground.

- ❖ Then, go back in your own footprints.

- ❖ Take your dog loosely on the leash and lead it through the track. Your dog will search with its eyes first.

- ❖ Now, kindly give it the command, 'Search!' while pointing to the ground.

❖ Praise your dog as soon as it lowers its nose onto the track on the ground.

❖ Praise it again when it sniffs and follows the track.

❖ Finally, praise it exuberantly when your dog finally finds the 'prey'.

❖ Make this track longer and longer over time until the object has finally disappeared completely from your dog's field of vision.

11. Mole game

Your dog will not want to dig in the flower bed anymore thanks to this game, because this is your remedy!

- ❖ Set aside a small corner in your garden and build a small sandpit there for your dog.

- ❖ Let it dig up treasures from the sand from time to time, such as toys or chew bones.

- ❖ In winter, your dog can dig things out of the snow there. The white version is as appealing to it as the sandy one.

12. Outdoor dog podium

Get your dog to climb onto a tree stump, a concrete block or a boulder and then reward it. If you want to, you can also practise getting your four-legged friend to run to the next tree stump or concrete block and climb it on your signal.

* It is easiest for your dog if you always practise on the same platform at first.

* Lure your dog onto the platform a few times in succession and reward it there.

* Think about which command you want to use for this exercise in the future, for example, 'Up!'. You should say your command immediately before you lure your dog onto the platform.

* While you are still close to your four-legged friend at first, step by step you will literally stay a little

further back and let your dog reach its goal on its own. If everything go-es well, with a little training you can send it to the platform from a few metres away eventually.

13. Action in the forest

Along the way, there are a lot of possibilities to train with your dog to use all of its legs in a coordinated way – even the hind legs!

- ❖ Lead your dog slowly over lying branches and thin tree trunks.

- ❖ Lead your dog in a zigzag over a very low fence again and again.

- ❖ Let it stomp through thick layers of leaves.

- ❖ If you often walk along the same forest path, remember a place on the other side of the path where you lay out a few branches in a ladder or fan shape.

- ❖ Walk your dog with your hand held low or spread a handful of food in the middle of your ground work elements so that your dog is automatically in action with all four legs when picking them up.

14. Walk in the woods

Not above but below, is the motto for a change.

- ❖ Let your dog crawl through the forest under branches and gnarled root pieces.

- ❖ Get it to cross under benches, barriers, bicycle stands or barrier chains.

15. Outdoor climbing fun

Especially when you are out in the woods with your four-legged friend, you can play this game.

- ❖ Let your dog climb up and down slopes and ramps.

- ❖ It will move particularly intensively if you spread a handful of food there and it is allowed to collect it on the obstacle.

- ❖ This also works well on stairs along the way.

16. Food track during the walk

There are many other ways to play with things along the way. For example, how about surprising your dog with a natural marble run?

❖ Let your dog wait at the foot of a ramp. Roll down food. Its task is to observe and catch the incoming food.

❖ Look for a shallow stream or trickle with little current. In front of your dog's eyes, drop a few unsinkable chunks of food (often dry food or thin dog cookies) into the water that are slowly carried away by the weak current. The task for your dog is to catch the crumbs, either from the edge or with all four legs in the stream.

17. Search the food bag

The dog learns to use its nose in a concentrated way and to hand off something very important for it, namely its food.

❖ Initially, put the dog on a chest harness and leash. Then, make a bag filled with treats attractive: throw it in the air and pull it back and forth on the ground. You can encourage your dog to tug at it. Reward your four-legged friend with food from the bag.

❖ Reward every little success!

❖ As soon as the interest in the bag is aroused, throw it a little further away. The dog may immediately follow. In the optimal case it picks it up. Praise this strongly and walk backwards. The dog must automatically follow you on the leash.

❖ When it arrives at your place, praise it, take the bag from it and reward it again with food from the bag. If necessary, pull the dog gently towards you.

❖ If the picking up and returning process works safely, you can start a first small search without the leash and introduce the audible and visual signal (for example, 'Bring!' and a corresponding arm movement in addition). First, you make the food bag attractive for the dog again.

❖ Then, you let it sit down. Now, place the bag about five metres away, slightly hidden. After the command, the dog may begin the search. When it has discovered the bag, show it that you are very happy about that and reward it with food from the bag as soon as it has brought it to you. If the returning process does not work yet, repeat the exercise with the drag line.

18. Follow the treat trail

A real favourite game of dogs who love to sniff. Here, their sense of smell is trained.

- ❖ Why not lay out a trail of small food crumbs for your dog?

- ❖ If it follows it, it will find a great reward at the end.

- ❖ If you play outside, you can pull a slice of pork sausage across the lawn.

- ❖ Then, take your dog to the beginning of your trail and see if it follows the scented trail – and finds the pork sausage at the end. You can also use a tube of dog liverwurst to dab a trail over rough and smooth surfaces outside.

Indoor games
– fun in the house
and in the apartment

1. Fishing game

First of all, you need a rope or a cord,
which should not be too thin so that your
dog can grip it well with its teeth. It is best
to make a thicker knot as a kind of grip on
one end.

❖ The treat waiting as a reward after
the work is done should be a bit
bigger so that you can easily attach
it to the other end of the rope. Chew
bones are particularly suitable.

❖ Do not make the knot too tight,
though, so that you can loosen it
quickly and easily.

❖ Now, all you need is something to

hide the treat and from which the rope is seen, looking like a fishing rod – for example a cupboard or a bed.

❖ Show your dog the treat and then place it in its hiding place so that only the rope is visible.

❖ The rope should not be too long at the beginning. If your dog has spotted the chew bone, it should not get it until you have released it from the rope. Therefore, you should not move too far away to be able to react quickly.

Variant:

If your dog gets the hang of it, you can increase the level of difficulty over time and place the treat on a longer rope further back under the piece of furniture.

2. Clever dogs distinguishing toys

Important: introduce each toy that you want to use later for the distinguishing game consistently with a single term. A ball – once it has been named 'ball' – must always remain 'ball', otherwise your dog will not understand you.

❖ In addition to precise communication, the ability to follow the commands, 'Search!' or 'Bring!' is required for this game.

- ❖ Start with a simple retrieving exercise and bring only one toy into play.

- ❖ Once your dog has successfully found it a few times, you can slowly increase the number of toys.

- ❖ In the next step, lay out different toys that can be easily distinguished from one another.

- ❖ Now, let your dog search for a certain toy and bring it to you. You must be patient: if your four-legged friend brings the wrong one, repeat the command. If it brings the right toy, reward it immediately with a treat.

3. Following gazes

This game is also primarily about your dog's ability to concentrate and combine. At the beginning, you should try out the game where your dog knows the place and feels safe so that it is not distracted. Later, you can try the training where there is more distraction, for example, outside.

❖ Your dog should be sitting quietly in front of you.

❖ Crouch down in front of it in such a way that you can spread out both arms well. In one hand you hold a hidden treat. Now, spread out both arms and turn your eyes and head very clearly towards the hand with the treat.

❖ Then, ask your dog to get the treat, for example, with the command, 'Get the treat!'.

❖ In doing so, observe your dog from the corners of your eyes.

❖ If it moves to the wrong hand first, ignore it and wait. If it finds it difficult to follow your gaze, it can be a great help to it if several people in the room look at the correct hand.

❖ Patience is important in this game. Allow your dog enough time to understand what you expect it to do. Practise only two or three times with the minimum requirement that the dog looks only slightly in the given direction. Later, you can wait for a clearer reaction. Finally, the dog should run to the right hand and pick up the treat.

4. Paws up! The somewhat different hurdle race

If you set up hurdles in your living room, don't do it so that they are jumped over. The space is usually too limited for this and the floor may be too slippery. Instead, the hurdles are overcome at walking pace, paw by paw. For the front paws this is usually no problem, but then it becomes difficult because many dogs have difficulties using their hind legs consciously. A nice challenge, and this is how it works:

❖ Suitable materials are, for example, brooms and scrubbing brushes with long handles, swimming noodles, rolled-up wool blankets, empty plastic flower boxes, thin PVC pipes or plastic planting sticks. The elements must be low enough for your dog to climb over them comfortably.

❖ First, try it out on a single object to see if you can get your dog to climb over it slowly.

❖ If in doubt, lay out a trail of food crumbs over the obstacle. If you show your dog the way with your hand, keep it very low.

5. Surfing adventure

What would your four-legged friend actually say if you spread a large plastic tarpaulin with many folds on the ground and guided your dog over it or invited it to play a food search game?

❖ Does it dare to do so when it suddenly becomes slippery under its feet and begins to rustle?

❖ The braver your dog is, the more the waves can pile up in your plastic sea, through which it has to fight its way.

Of course, you must always keep an eye on your dog not getting caught in the piled up tarpaulin.

6. Tactile gangway

To march fearlessly and safely over the most varied surfaces is practical for everyday life and a great adventure for your living room parkour. You can build a tactile gangway out of different materials.

❖ Suitable materials are, for example, doormats of different structures, plastic bags and sacks, pieces of carpet, newspaper, aluminum foil, shower mats, large pieces of cardboard and folded boxes, a piece of polystyrene, a rolled-up wool blanket, a shelf, garden chair cushions or similar.

❖ Depending on your dog's courage, you first start to deal with the elements individually before stringing them together.

❖ Try to get your dog to actually put all four paws (simultaneously or one after the other) onto the unfamiliar material. Especially if it is unsure, celebrate and reward every step, no matter how small.

❖ Before the tactile gang walk is crossed completely, let your dog conquer each surface individually. All four paws should have come into contact with the material once.

7. Wobbling air mattress

Take an air mattress and inflate it so that it gets half-full. If the air mattress is very thin and slippery, wrap it up in a wool blanket. Then, your dog may conquer the wobbly air mattress.

- ❖ At the beginning, try to get your dog to only put one or two paws on the mattress – for example, when it is angling for a small piece of food lying on the mattress. It should be able to gently experience that it now wobbles under its paws and that it sinks in a little.

- ❖ Your next goal is to get your four-legged friend to cross the air mattress, for example, by following a food track. The easiest way to do this is to first march over the mattress crosswise and then lengthwise.

- ❖ The finale. Your dog gets on the

mattress with all four paws, stands on it (sits or lies down) and balances itself. Try to encourage it to shift its weight slightly. For example, you could put a piece of food in front of its paws or ask it to sit or lie down.

In any case, reward and praise it effusively while it is on the mattress.

8. The rustling curtain

Does your dog dare to march through a curtain consisting of hanging objects?

* ❖ Stretch a rope between two chair backs; alternatively, tie a broom handle to the backs. This is your basic framework for the test of courage.

* ❖ Attach a curtain of hanging cloths, newspaper strips or barrier tape to the rope or bar.

* ❖ If you enjoy handicrafts, you can also string beer coasters, cardboard rolls or old CDs on cords and attach them to your basic frame.

* ❖ Can you manage to get your dog to go through this curtain?

    This is the easiest way to do it:

* ❖ At first, it should not take your dog much effort to push the curtain aside. Therefore, start with very few,

light and quiet elements.

❖ Spread a few food crumbs so that they are under the curtain, in front of it and behind it. Your dog will get used to coming into contact with the elements of the curtain and will even find it 'delicious'. If your dog likes to run under the curtain more often to look for food, then you have done everything right.

9. Cleaning up and learning vocabulary

If your dog likes to retrieve, you can even teach it vocabulary!

- ❖ Take a ball from its toy box and put it on the floor in front of the dog.

- ❖ Sit next to it, point to the ball and tell your dog to 'Bring me the ball!'.

- ❖ Praise it when it arrives with the plaything.

- ❖ Now, point to the box and give it the command, 'Drop it!'.

- ❖ Reward your dog when it drops the ball into the toy box.

- ❖ Now, choose two toys with different names, for example, 'rope' and 'ball'. Ask your dog again to bring you one of the toys. Give it great praise when it grabs the right one!

- ❖ Over time, you can gradually increase the number of toys you want your dog to put in the toy box.

10. Labyrinth

This game can be played both indoors and outdoors.

- ❖ Place poles, broom handles and swimming noodles on the floor to create a labyrinth.

- ❖ Now, lead your dog through these corridors by holding a treat in front of its mouth.

- ❖ Praise it when it walks nicely along the corridors without touching the boundaries. Of course, it will get big praise and its treat at the end!

- ❖ Later on, your dog should be led through the labyrinth without any treats – for example, only by hand signals!

11. The game with the kitchen roll

This game promotes the playing instinct of your dog.

- ❖ First of all, take a kitchen roll or a toilet roll.

- ❖ Place it on a kitchen roll holder or hold the roll between your hands.

- ❖ Now, encourage your dog to unroll the paper from the roll either with its paws or with its nose.

- ❖ Practise in small steps and reward your dog as soon as it touches the roll.

- ❖ Finally, get it to unroll the paper at your command.

  The unrolled kitchen paper can be folded together again and used to wipe kitchen surfaces.

12. Cleaning the paws

This game makes your everyday life easier. First of all, you need a doormat.

- ❖ Position your four-legged friend with its front paws on the doormat.

- ❖ Now, take one of the paws in your hand and pull it carefully over the mat.

- ❖ Give your dog a command of your choice like, 'Wipe your paws!', and reward it.

- ❖ Then, take the other paw and repeat the procedure.

- ❖ Practise this until your dog has understood exactly what it has to do and wipes its paws independently at your command.

- ❖ You can also practise this with its hind paws.

13. Game for two – jump on the back

Your dog learns to coordinate its jumping movement so well that it lands safely on your back and balances itself there.

❖ Your starting position is the all-fours position; your dog sits in front of the side of your body. A second person should now get the dog to approach your back and finally jump onto it. To do this, your helper stands opposite the dog on the other side and lures it towards your back with a treat in his hand.

❖ This exercise is easy to implement with a clicker and target stick. It goes like this: the helper holds the target stick against your back. As soon as the dog touches the stick, there is a click.

❖ Put the stick higher gradually until the dog touches your back with its front paws and finally jumps. Now, you can introduce the appropriate command. To prevent the dog from simply jumping over your back or immediately jumping down again, the assisting person can stand so close to your back that he represents a natural boundary for the dog.

14. The perfect bow

With this task, the dog trains its coordination and attentiveness.

- ❖ In the starting position, the dog stands in front of you.

- ❖ In the first step, the dog should put its head on the ground. In order for it to do so, lure it with a food reward. Your four-legged friend gets the treat if it follows your hand with its snout down to the floor – then, it receives big praise.

- ❖ In order for the dog to actually bow in the second step, don't be satisfied with it just taking its head down. First, lure it down again with the hand with the treat, but do not yet give it the food reward, but push the hand carefully under its snout, towards the dog's front paws.

- ❖ In order to get the treat, the dog must now lower itself down to its front legs – and for this it gets big praise and of course the treat. It is possible that your dog will go from this position straightaway into the lying down position. In this case, your timing is important. Praise it exactly when it is lying on its elbows so that it links the reward to exactly this position.

❖ When it has understood this, you can introduce the appropriate command, for example, 'Take a bow!'. Important: terminate the bow with your usual termination command. This command must come quickly, especially at the beginning, so that the dog does not lie down.

15. Get the cap

Coordination and independent working are in the foreground of this funny trick. The close interaction promotes bonding.

- ❖ At first, the dog should learn to grasp the cap at the visor with its mouth. To do this, crouch down and put the cap in front of your dog.

- ❖ You don't need to give it a signal, just wait until it sniffs curiously at the cap. For this, it gets a click and a treat.

- ❖ Repeat this a few times and then take a longer break before you do the whole procedure again (maybe not until the next day).

- ❖ If the dog has understood that it is about the cap, practise the next step with it.

- ❖ Now, it should pick up the cap with its mouth. Therefore, do not click anymore when the dog touches the cap with its snout, but wait. In this way, the dog will notice that mere sniffing is no longer sufficient and will offer stronger actions. As soon as it picks up the cap with its mouth, click – until it has understood this, too.

❖ Now, it goes upwards. Put the cap on your head, at the beginning still so loose that it can be pulled down easily. Then, you bend towards the dog a little bit until it gets the idea to sniff at the cap – click and reward.

❖ After that, you build up the action step by step until the dog pulls the cap off your head. Using the clicker principle this can succeed very quickly. As soon as the dog masters a step safely – for example, it takes the cap in its mouth – you do not click anymore, but wait until it pulls it more strongly. In return, it will get a click again until this works easily.

Enter the signal words as soon as the exercise works, for example, 'Get the cap!'.

16. Scent game for real sniffers

If your dog's talent for smelling is still dormant, this game will teach it to use its sense of smell with concentration.

❖ First, familiarise your dog with the scent you want to use for this game.

❖ Put a drop of it on a cloth and play with it together with your dog. After this preparation, the nose work begins. Prepare a paper towel with the scent and place it on the floor in front of the dog. The dog may sniff at it extensively. Now, your reaction is decisive. As if the dog has just found something that you have been missing for a long time, pick up the tissue, smell it and be very happy about it.

❖ Now, try the whole procedure with two cloths.

❖ One contains a drop of scent, the other does not.

❖ Let the dog smell both cloths.

❖ Praise it effusively if it reacts to the right cloth for a moment longer than for the other cloth, for example, by smelling at it or picking it up. After a few repetitions, the dog will understand that it should find the scent. If it hasn't understood it yet or if it regularly tears the cloths apart, use a little trick: put each cloth deep into a narrow, empty jam jar or a tall drinking glass.

❖ Observe how your dog indicates the paper with the scent. Does it pick up the cloth? Is it touching it with its paw? Or does it simply remain longer at the right cloth? You can support its right behaviour with the clicker.

❖ You should not train this game in only one day. Give the dog time for the individual steps. Practise from time to time.

17. Dream blanket with food bonus

During this game, your four-legged friend can sniff and earn treats at the same time. Its sense of smell is also trained.

- ❖ Put old wool blankets or towels on the floor.

- ❖ Hide food crumbs in the folds of the blanket and let your master sniffer search for them.

18. Dinner in the dark

Sniffing and rewards do not come up short here.

- ❖ You put some food crumbs in a darkened room, turn off the light and send your dog searching.

- ❖ With a little practice, and if your four-legged friend knows a signal word for the search for food, it will later surely find even tiny treats in the pitch-dark room effortlessly.

- ❖ By the way, the same game also works very well on dark winter evenings when going for a walk or in the garden.

Food games

Food games are mainly about dexterity and about the dog having to test when and how quickly it can get its food. For example, treats that have been hidden can be used here so that your dog, with the appropriate concentration, can figure out how to get the food. Most dogs have a lot of fun with food games because there is always a tasty reward when the game is successfully implemented.

It won't get boring because there are many different possibilities for food games, which are a challenge to the skill of the dog – a little patience on the part of the dog can't hurt neither.

For these food games and unpacking games, you need utensils like towels, boxes, plastic bottles and of course treats. These games are great for happy minutes in between. You don't need a long preparation time and your four-legged friend will certainly have a lot of fun!

1. Licking ice cream

Do you love ice cream? Your dog does, too – especially on hot summer days! It's best to use a Kong for this and ideally fill it with yogurt ice cream. This will provide your dog with a special treat on hot days, and it can lick its very own ice cream together with you.

❖ Freeze the previously filled Kong for a few hours.

❖ Now you can give the Kong with the frozen content to your dog. This is best done outside in the garden or on a meadow to save yourself the cleaning work afterwards.

❖ You can mix a bit of liver sausage into the yogurt before freezing, depending on the taste and preferences of your dog.

2. Treat ball game

Simple, well-known and easy to implement is the game with the treat ball, which you can buy in any pet store. The balls have a special opening into which treats or pieces of food are filled. The balls are made from quite different materials for the respective preference of the dog. This is probably the best-known food game.

- ❖ Put the food ball on the floor and enjoy the spectacle.

- ❖ After a short sniff, your dog will try to get the treats from inside the ball to the outside. Your dog may not immediately understand which technique will lead it to the goal the fastest.

- ❖ Therefore, choose a very large opening the first time so that your dog does not give up in frustration.

- ❖ Once it has understood what it is all about, your dog will develop its individual strategy. Some dogs kick the ball, while others throw it around or turn it gently to one side so that the coveted reward rolls out.

Tip:

If you use a food ball made of hard plastic in the house, you should ensure that nothing can break in the playing area. It could get tumultuous!

3. Joy of unpacking

Not only humans like to unwrap gifts, the same goes for dogs! You can gift-wrap treats and then make your dog unwrap them. You don't need much for this game as you can simply wrap up treats in newspaper – or use other sheets of paper that you no longer need.

- ❖ Start by wrapping up individual treats, and in the next step, wrap up the individual packages into a larger package. This adds to the challenge and keeps your dog busy with a tricky task – let the fun of unwrapping begin!

- ❖ You may need to provide encouragement by opening a small piece of the package first. After that, the dog will quickly understand how to properly unwrap the gifts and what awaits it afterwards.

4. Chew games

Nowadays, chew toys are offered in pet shops in a variety of forms and with many different notches and degrees of difficulty. The best known representative is the Kong.

❖ The principle is quite simple: various treats can be stuffed into a rubber toy with small openings. Your dog must now bring them to the light of day with concentrated chewing, skillful use of its tongue and a lot of patience.

❖ Depending on the type of toy, you can be creative and use treats made of different ingredients and in different consistencies. Spreads suitable for dogs make this game a real gourmet party for your dog.

❖ Allow your four-legged friend a little fun with a chew toy from time to time. Concentrated chewing not only cares for the teeth, the monotonous activity is the purest relaxation for your dog. Last, but not least, chew games are exciting character studies in themselves. Every dog has its own way of chewing – tender, rather rough or almost meditative.

Tip:

Dogs that are regularly given the opportunity to chew on a chew toy feel less of an urge to nibble on furniture, children's toys and shoes. Very useful and practical!

5. Shell game

Plastic cones are available in pet shops, but you can also look for suitable plastic cups in department stores or toy shops. An inexpensive alternative is, for example, rinsed yogurt cups.

❖ This game is about letting your four-legged friend find a treat under a set of plastic cones. It might not understand that right at the beginning. Therefore, start with a small selection, i.e. only one cone. Show your dog the treat and place it under one of the cones.

❖ Your dog will now sniff at the cone and try to get the treat underneath. It can either push it down with its nose or paw or put it aside with its mouth. If your dog does not immediately understand what to do, just show it the treat again and again and put it back under the cone.

❖ Once your dog gets the hang of it, you can make the game more complicated. Set up a set of cones and let your dog find the one with the treat. You can interchange the cones after you have hidden the treat.

6. Where is it?

This play promotes, in particular, the sense of smell of your four-legged friend.

- ❖ Take a treat in one hand and now clench both hands into a fist.

- ❖ Hold out both hands to your dog and ask it where the treat is hiding.

- ❖ Some dogs just test out, others rely on their sense of smell.

- ❖ Once your dog has decided on a hand, open it.

- ❖ If the treat is inside, your dog can have it.

- ❖ If the treat is not in there, show your dog the treat in the other hand.

- ❖ Then, close both hands again and ask again where the treat is. Let your dog try again.

- ❖ If you want to make this game more

difficult, you can play it with more people. Sit next to each other. One person has the treat in his hand and the dog can actively sniff and search for it.

7. Adventure games in the forest

With this game you strengthen, on the one hand, the bond between your dog and you and on the other hand, the self-confidence of your four-legged friend.

- ❖ Go into the forest with your dog.

- ❖ Now, hide some treats in a pile of leaves. You can also place a treat under branches or bushes.

- ❖ Then, let your dog search for the reward.

- ❖ Has it found it? In this case it may eat the prey!

- ❖ The rustling leaves should awaken your dog's spirit of adventure and joy of playing.

- ❖ You can also search for the prey together with your dog. This strengthens the bond between you!

8. Exploring pots

This food game is also extremely popular with dogs!

- ❖ Let your dog sit down and give it a treat to sniff at.

- ❖ Now, place some jars, such as plastic bowls, rinsed yogurt cups or flower pots, upside down on the floor.

- ❖ Then, place the treat under a jar in front of your dog's eyes and give your dog the command, 'Okay, go get it!'.

- ❖ Praise it when it has sniffed out the right jar and is able to tip it over with its snout or paws.

- ❖ Later on, it must not watch while you are hiding the treat but must find out for itself under which jar the treat is lying.

9. The safe-breaker

❖ Put small treats or dry food in a cardboard box and seal it with some tape.

❖ Cut or prick some holes into the box.

❖ Give this 'safe' to your dog and tell it, 'Okay' in an encouraging way.

❖ Praise your four-legged friend as soon as it succeeds in getting the delicious content out of the box – either by chewing up the cardboard box or getting the treats through the holes.

10. The 'rock 'n' roll' game

❖ Unscrew the top of an empty PET bottle and put dry food into the bottle.

❖ Now, lay the bottle on the floor.

❖ Your dog should then try to get the treats out of the bottle by rolling and shaking it. This is dog's 'rock 'n' roll'!

11. Role playing – somewhat different

Do not throw away the cardboard roll of the toilet paper immediately because from it you can conjure up a great game for y-our four-legged friend.

- ❖ Put a treat into the cardboard roll and press the ends together.

- ❖ Now, give the roll to your dog.

- ❖ It may then shred it to its heart's content to get to the tasty filling.

- ❖ Praise your dog if it manages to get to the content.

- ❖ You don't necessarily have to put in ready-made food, you can also put in chopped chicken meat.

12. Nose acrobatics

❖ With a 'Catch!' command, throw a treat to your dog, which it must catch with its mouth.

❖ As soon as this works perfectly, give your dog the command, 'Sit!'. Now, place a small treat on the bridge of its nose.

❖ And again, the signal, 'Catch!' follows.

❖ After some time, skilled dogs will indeed succeed in letting the treat fly up with a short head bounce and then snap it up from the air.

This is not so easy!

❖ If this succeeds, your four-legged friend will get huge praise!

Diving and water games

In these games the rewards are distributed at the bottom of a water basin. Here, your dog must fish out the treats with its paws or mouth. Such games should only be played outside to avoid flooding in the house or apartment. Especially in summer, these games are a real pleasure – whether in the stream, on the lakeshore or in the dog paddling pool in your garden. Instead of a treat, toys can, of course, also be hidden at the bottom of the water.

TIP against the summer heat:

Make a towel wet, wring it out and let your four-legged friend lie under or on top of it for a moment – of course, in the shade, please!

If you like, you can also buy a cooling mat to make the heat more bearable for your pet.

1. Diving game with treats

Depending on the size of your dog, bowls, plastic tubs for children or large buckets are suitable containers for this game. The game itself is simple: you sink the treat in the water – your dog has to save it.

❖ It is best to practise with a low fill level first. Not every dog is a lover of water. Some of them have to overcome themselves to stick their snout into the cold water. So, don't give up in frustration if it doesn't work right away!

❖ Show your dog the treat before you sink it. Once your dog gets the hang of it and knows what's important, you can gradually increase the fill level of the container.

❖ You can integrate this game perfectly into a parkour with other game elements, which you can run through together with other dog owners and their four-legged friends.

Tip:

For this refreshing fun bath – possibly not only for the dog – use lukewarm water, never ice-cold water!

2. Ball game 'diving down'

This game trains, on the one hand, the attentiveness, and on the other hand, the condition of your dog.

- ❖ The dog is allowed to swim in the water, for example, in a lake.

- ❖ Now, give several balls to your dog in the water – but one after the other!

- ❖ A hard rubber ball sinks. If the lake is not too shallow, this can be turned into a fun diving game. The dog should dive down and bring the ball back to you.

- ❖ Lighter balls float on the water's surface.

- ❖ Give your dog an appropriate signal to retrieve the ball.

By the way, you can find special balls for

diving games in specialist shops. They sink and stay on the bottom but are not too heavy for dogs.

Tips for playing in the water:

There are many dogs that like to play and retrieve in the water. But there are some rules to be observed:

- ❖ Start with a ball in shallow water. As soon as this works well, you can throw the ball into deeper spots.

- ❖ Do not overdo it with water games and take breaks regularly.

- ❖ Dogs with osteoarthritis should not enter too cold water because cold intensifies joint pain.

- ❖ Dogs with epilepsy should never be allowed to enter too deep water, because during an epileptic seizure the danger of drowning would be much too great.

❖ When swimming, dogs use their tail; this can quickly lead to sore muscles. Therefore, take sufficient breaks!

❖ After bathing in colder temperatures, you should always dry your dog because otherwise there is a risk of it becoming hypothermic and catching a cold.

3. Fishing dog

Is no puddle safe from your four-legged friend? Then why not treat him to a nice shallow paddling pool in a small garden corner. Just like smaller children, he will love it.

- ❖ Let your dog fish toys or treats out of it again and again.

- ❖ This is great bathing fun, especially for lovers of water who also like to retrieve.

4. Water parkour

Water is an Eldorado for the fans of the dog parkour. Whether a clear puddle or a fountain, a trickle or a stream, you and your dog can have a lot of fun there. Get your four-legged friend to go into the cool water with all four paws and then wade a little through it.

❖ Practise in a clean shallow puddle or a narrow stream. The water should only be a few centimetres deep.

❖ Take a piece of food and place it, for example, on a stone or directly in the water in such a way that your dog only has to put one paw into the water to get to it.

❖ Once it has successfully managed this step a few times, the demands will be somewhat increased. To get to the food, it then has to put two paws into the water; later on, all four. And at some point, the food crumbs lie so that the dog even has to walk a few steps, first in shallow water, then a little deeper.

❖ Very important: always be patient and resist the temptation to simply take your dog and put it down in the water. This would only increase its aversion to the cool water.

Intelligence
and brain games

Not all games have something to do with coordination, agility or sniffing out prey. Also, intelligence games are very popular, or those where dogs have to show what they can achieve mentally. The advantage of the brain games is that you don't need a big park or a garden for them. So, a lot is possible in your own four walls.

These games promote your dog's intelligence, creativity and mental workout. Try out which games go down well with your dog. By the way, many games in this category are ideal if your dog is no longer in top physical shape, or simply if you want to encourage real brainwork. After all, brain jogging is not only beneficial and extremely useful for us humans to stay mentally sharp.

However, these games can be exhausting because just as with humans, this applies to animals: thinking is exhausting. For this reason, an optimal combination of tricky tasks and sufficient breaks is needed.

1. Finding the right object

This game trains the power of deduction and the ability to concentrate.

Your four-legged friend should know some of its toys by name, for example, ball, rope, bone, rabbit, bear, etc.

❖ You practise this by placing a toy in front of your dog and calling it by name just before it picks it up with its mouth.

❖ You can also use the clicker as a reinforcement.

❖ Later, you ask your dog to bring you the toy in question and click or praise it strongly when it hands it over to you. Of course, there is a reward for this.

❖ For dogs that do not like to pick up objects, a nudge is enough. In this way, many dogs quickly learn to know some toys by name.

2. Head-shaking

This game can be played both indoors and outdoors and does not require any special preparation. This game can also be very useful in everyday life.

- ❖ Take a treat in your hand and hold it in front of your dog's nose.

- ❖ Now, move your hand a little to the left and then to the right.

- ❖ If your dog follows your hand with its head, give the command, 'Say no!' and reward it.

- ❖ Repeat this process until your dog has understood which movement is to be made without having to hold the treat in front of its nose.

3. Shell game - somewhat different

A shell game with a completely different focus – in the truest sense of the word.

❖ For a change, experiment with cones that your dog cannot easily knock over. Flat bowls, for example, are well suited for this.

❖ Lay a treat under one of them in front of your dog's eyes and see what your four-legged friend is doing. Does it skillfully push the bowl into a corner and lift it up there with its nose? Does it step on the edge with its paws and in this way get under it with its nose? It will probably develop completely new techniques.

4. Stacking game

For brave dogs and those who want to become one.

- ❖ You build a tower and hide food in the storeys. The task of your dog is to bring everything down.

- ❖ Ideal for this are stacking cups for children or you build a stack of bowls, boxes and cups. Toilet paper rolls (with or without paper on them) are also suitable for this. Do not overdo it with the height.

- ❖ Only play on noise-reducing surfaces, for example, on the carpet, on a wool blanket or on the lawn.

- ❖ Very important: never start with a complete tower, but only with two low elements between which a piece of food is placed. Only when your dog brings this mini stack down safely and enthusiastically, can you add on more elements. Add a third element, in combination with an additional piece of food. Only when the combination of three elements is just as well overturned again and again, the fourth element is added and so on.

5. Premium shell game

This is a real challenge for experienced thimbleriggers because it requires a lot of problem-solving skills and stamina. This time, the cone stands the other way round, i.e. with the opening to the top, and it is also very high.

❖ How high the cone has to be depends on the size of your dog. Your dog should not be able to look over the upper edge into the interior when standing. Large boxes or buckets are well suited for this.

❖ In front of your dog's eyes, drop a dog cookie – clearly audibly – into the box or bucket.

❖ Then, it is your dog's turn. Will it manage to knock the box or bucket over and then get to the piece of food inside?

❖ Just in case all your dog's efforts come to nothing, cut the box a little

shorter or tilt it slightly so that your
dog can knock it over better.

6. Cardboard box game for good noses

There are lids to remove, lids to open, lids to unfold. And all this in a wide variety of sizes and textures, from small tea bag boxes to shoe boxes to large postal parcels. Every variation can be a challenge for your dog. Put in the treats, close the lid and off you go!

❖ First, let your dog eat a piece of food from the open box. This is how it learns that there is food in there; I want to go in there!

❖ Now, the lid comes into play. First, you close it only halfway (leave it open a little bit or just put it loosely over the opening) so that your dog can still easily reach the food. It will already get used to the fact that a lid is in the way.

❖ After that, close the lid bit by bit, more and more. Slide it further over the opening or let the gap of the lid become narrower. Your dog now has the chance to learn how the opening mechanism works.

❖ Now comes the exciting moment: the lid is completely closed. Hold the box tightly and trust your dog that it will be able to solve this task.

7. Opening food storage boxes

If your dog already has had a little practice in opening packages, it will probably also be able to use pursed lips to remove the lid of a food storage box if there is a piece of food in it.

❖ First, place the lid loosely on the box. Your dog only needs to push it to the side to reach the contents.

❖ Once your dog has understood the principle (remove the lid to get to the food), close the lid but leave a gap open on one side. This allows your dog to use its snout or paw to lift the lid.

❖ If this also works, close the lid completely. Make it easier for your dog by holding the box firmly in your hands.

8. The safe champion

If your dog is already an experienced safe-breaker, surprise it now and then with covers that work completely differently than the usual opening mechanisms.

* ❖ To do this, place food in a box, case or bucket and lay a blanket or towel over it. Inflate a water polo ball just enough to cover the opening with it, clog the opening with a toy and hang a kitchen sieve in the opening. Get a little creative here.

* ❖ Then, let your dog take out the treat.

* ❖ Do not forget to praise and reward it.

9. Rolling board

Using household objects as mental exercise devices has a great advantage: they are ideal for experimenting a little with them and offering variety to the dog, and afterwards they can be returned to normal use. Plant rollers and furniture dollies are a good example of this. Yesterday a plant roller, today a mental exercise device.

❖ Place a piece of food underneath so that your dog cannot reach it with its snout.

❖ What does your Einstein do? Does it find the solution directly and push the board away? Does it first walk around the rolling board and look at the situation from all sides? When sniffing for the food, does it discover, by chance, that the board is movable? Whatever the case, give it the chance for several repetitions so that it can perfect its system.

❖ Does your dog have no idea what to do with the rolling board or does it not dare to push it aside? Then put the food underneath it during the first attempts so that it can still reach the food with its tongue initially. Centimetre by centimetre the food moves further under the board with each new attempt.

10. Clever search for food

Is there a stable shelf, cupboard or sofa in your apartment that has feet just high enough to leave a narrow gap to the floor? Your dog's body and head will not fit under this gap, but its paws will? Then you can look forward to another brain jogging challenge.

- ❖ Put a piece of food under the shelf in front of your dog's eyes and see what your dog does. It will soon see that it can't do anything with its snout. Will it get the idea to fish for it with its paws?

- ❖ If that doesn't work right away, design the first attempts so that your dog can reach the food with its snout at first and put it a little further back from time to time.

- ❖ Motivated by its first successes, it will probably try more and more to get to the food.

11. Special search for food

This time, you let food disappear in a drawer. No problem for your dog, which will open it again.

How to make the automat:

* ❖ Get a cookie package: its inner part is pulled out of the outer packaging like a drawer. Eat the cookies or store them somewhere else.

* ❖ Attach a loop to the drawer by first cutting a slit in the end of the drawer. You can create a handy tab by pushing a strip of masking tape or insulating tape through the slit (the adhesive sides on top of each other so that the dog's nose does not get stuck on it later). Alternatively, you can fasten a piece of cloth with knots in the slit.

How your dog cracks the mechanism:

- ❖ Sit down in front of your dog. Place a food crumb in the front of the cookie package before your dog's eyes.

- ❖ Do not close the drawer completely at first. Leave a gap open in which your dog's nose will just fit.

- ❖ Hold the package out to your dog at about the height of its snout.

- ❖ When the dog bores into the gap with its nose, it will reach the piece of food. The learning effect: there is food in the drawer, and I have to put my nose into the drawer!

- ❖ Let the gap get smaller and smaller so that your dog has to make more and more effort to push its nose into the gap and thus open the drawer.

- ❖ Observe your dog carefully. As soon as the nose hardly fits into the gap, the moment will come when your dog will use its teeth to pull the drawer open. If it has this good idea, help quickly, if in doubt.

❖ Is your dog doing a good job? Then put the food in the very back of the drawer so that it has to be pulled out completely.

12. Intelligent downpipe

An ideal brain game for your four-legged friend. If it is already familiar with other games, it will certainly enjoy this one.

How to make a downpipe:

- ❖ You will need a cardboard tube (for example, of kitchen paper, wrapping paper or aluminum foil) and additionally some stable cardboard.

- ❖ Use a carpet knife or scissors to cut two opposite horizontal slits in the upright tube. Cut a strip of cardboard so that you can push it straight through the slits of the tube and it still has enough overhang on both sides. Your design is just right for the beginning when the cardboard can be pushed or pulled through the slits with almost no resistance. If this doesn't work, enlarge the slits accordingly.

- ❖ If you now throw a food chunk into

the vertically held tube, it will remain on the cardboard strip inside the tube.

How to get your dog to pull on the strip:

- ❖ Does your dog already know how to pull on things from other games, for example, tug of war? Then try to encourage it to pull on the cardboard strip.

- ❖ Put the strip in your hand first and reward your dog when it takes it or pulls on it.

- ❖ In the middle of the flow of the exercise, insert the strip loosely into the slit of the tube – without food in it yet. Reward your dog strongly when it pulls on it again. If your dog does a good job, push the strip completely through the tube. Now, you can fill in food, which will fall out of the bottom of the tube.

13. Marble run

To further boost your creativity.

* With a little imagination you can create great constructions that will inspire you and your dog. For example, how about a marble run for your dog, a tube construction made of drainpipes or transparent pond hoses? You throw in round, easily rollable food chunks at the top and your dog will see or hear them rolling down.

* This is not so much a mental exercise as a dog surprise, but you and your dog will have a lot of fun with it. And if the tubes are big enough and you want to make more out of them, why not teach your dog to throw the balls into them itself?

14. Give me your paw

This little trick requires dexterity above all else.

- ❖ The first step is to teach the dog to lift its front paws to the level of its head, for example, like this: you let the dog sit down, take a treat in y-our hand and run your hand over its snout until it finally tries to get at it with one paw. If it touches your raised hand with its paw, it gets the treat as a reward.

- ❖ If the dog has understood the mo-vement in principle, practise the same with the other paw.

- ❖ If this works on both sides, practise now without treats in the respective hand. If the dog puts its paw in the palm of your hand, it will get the treat from the other hand. Train both sides until this works well. Don't practise the individual steps too often but build up the movement sequences slowly – two or three times per round are enough.

15. Searching for treats in the towel

The sense of smell, patience and dexterity are trained through this game.

❖ In order to give your dog a sense of achievement as quickly as possible at the beginning, do not hide the treat so deep inside the rolled-up towel at first, but a little further towards the front. Now, the dog should use its snout or paw.

❖ The dog starts to experiment to find out which technique promises the desired success.

❖ Let it try it out in peace and quiet for the time being. Praise it extensively in between because it shows so much patience and endurance.

❖ Later, you can start to roll the treat deeper and deeper into the towel to increase the level of difficulty until the entire towel must be spread out before the dog gets the desired treat.

16. Catching the treat

Discipline and dexterity are required here because the dog must wait calmly until the signal comes to catch the treat – then it may catch it in the air with a lot of skillfulness.

- ❖ It is a prerequisite that the dog remains in the sitting position because first of all it has to stay calm with the treat on its nose.

- ❖ The first step is to teach your four-legged friend to leave the treat on its nose.

- ❖ To do this, carefully encompass its snout and place the treat far forwards on your dog's nose. If your dog withstands this even for a moment, take the treat off its nose and give it to it as a reward for its patience.

- ❖ Now, you need to increase its stamina to a few seconds. Try it two or three times in a row and repeat this exercise for a few days until the dog reliably waits with the reward on its nose.

❖ Then, we come to the next step. Think of a short signal or sound, for example, 'Throw!' or 'Catch!'. A loud snap of the fingers also serves this purpose.

❖ Place the treat on the dog's nose as described above and position yourself two steps in front of the dog.

❖ Now, call out your command or snap your fingers and make an encouraging arm movement upwards. With a bit of luck, the dog will throw its head up and try to catch the treat.

❖ If this doesn't work at first, pick up the treat and try again.

❖ Don't repeat the attempts more than two or three times and don't forget to praise your four-legged friend extensively – even if the trick hasn't worked yet.

Balancing games

In this type of game, gymnastic balls are moved over a surface. The ball, which is permanently in motion, helps your four-legged friend to learn to control its body much better.

Therefore, balancing games are excellent for training the equilibrium.

1. Seesaw for dogs

With a non-slip board, you can promote your dog's balance and body coordination. The seesaw for dogs is also a special test of courage.

- ❖ Wrap a wide shelf board into an anti-slip mat (for example, a rug pad).

- ❖ Slide a crumpled up wool blanket or a folded bath towel under the board. At the beginning, it should only wobble very slightly.

- ❖ Get your dog to put one or two paws on the board. Reward it for that and then lead it down again.

- ❖ If it is not too wobbly, it may even dare to use all four paws on the seesaw. Don't forget the reward for this great balancing act!

2. Balancing game for professionals

This game is of medium to high difficulty and only something for real patience professionals. It promotes body awareness, concentration, coordination, patience and the dexterity of your dog.

❖ Take some dog cookies and stack them on your dog's nose or head.

(Your dog should already know this step and have done it several times before.)

The dog should stand and not sit when stacking.

❖ Now, the dog should carefully walk forwards with the stacked cookies.

❖ Reward each movement of your four-legged friend, no matter how small, with your voice.

❖ Practise this balancing exercise until your dog can easily walk a few steps without losing the cookies.

❖ Once it has reached its destination – for example, you – it can eat the cookies.

3. The hammock

This game particularly trains the sense of balance of your four-legged friend. It should not be played with very old dogs. They have a worse sense of balance and therefore a higher risk of injury.

❖ Attach a hammock between two chairs.

❖ Now, lure your dog into the hammock with a treat.

❖ Fix the hammock during the first jumps so that it does not rock too much.

❖ Once your four-legged friend has learned to jump into the hammock without any problems, you can set the hammock in motion before the jump.

❖ Reward the dog after each jump into the hammock!

4. Being an elephant – a game for bigger and heavy dogs

For this game you need a robust box. With this game you train above all the dexterity and the sense of balance of your dog.

* ❖ Place a solid box on the floor.

* ❖ First of all, make your four-legged friend familiar with the box.

* ❖ Now, encourage it to put its front paws on the box.

* ❖ If this works well, make sure you reward your dog with a treat!

* ❖ Then, let the dog climb all the way onto the box.

* ❖ In the next step, encourage it to get on the ground with its front paws. The hind paws should remain on the box.

* ❖ Reward your dog for this great performance!

5. Jello

Here, the dexterity and balance of your dog are required. If it can do this, it will gain a good dose of self-confidence!

- ❖ Build a seesaw from a long board with a rough surface and a short, thick piece of wood (for example, a piece of firewood).

- ❖ Lead your leashed dog onto the board and let it stand at the tipping point.

- ❖ Now, tilt the board by hand.

- ❖ The next time you do this, lead your four-legged friend through in one go. It will notice for itself that it can make the seesaw tilt.

- ❖ Please stop immediately when you see that your pet is afraid! However, most dogs are happy about the jello game and quickly manage the task, even without a leash.

Conclusion

Thank you very much for choosing this book.

I hope that you have been able to take a lot of valuable new information with you. There are numerous creative game ideas, which you can vary according to your own ideas and the preferences of your four-legged friend. Just try out the games and enjoy an unforgettable time together. You can also incorporate games into the daily walk and in this way bring a lot of variety into your everyday life.

Look for 'toys' you find in daily life from time to time: empty packaging and leaves or old blankets offer many exciting possibilities for fun hours of play. Your dog will certainly not get bored!

Finally, one thing is particularly important to emphasise: do not forget to relax with your furry friend while playing and romping around. Relaxing is just as important for your dog as the activity and fun of playing. In order to be really satisfied, healthy and balanced, dogs need sufficient hours of rest. So, allow your dog with a clear conscience to enjoy some relaxing hours – especially together with you. Make yourself comfortable on the couch and cuddle it on a blanket. Regular massages and stroking will increase the well-being of your dog and, of course, yours! At the same time, you will build a strong and trusting bond with your dog.

No matter whether you are relaxing, playing or romping, I wish you a successful and wonderful time with your four-legged friend!

Did you like the book?

Dear reader,

Are you satisfied with the book? Were your expectations fulfilled?

Then I look forward to your feedback, praise, criticism and suggestions.

Therefore, I would be pleased if you would leave me feedback on Amazon so that I can improve even further.

Many thanks in advance.

Sina Eschenweber

Disclaimer

The implementation of all information, instructions and strategies contained in this book is at your own risk. The author cannot be held liable for any damages of any kind for any legal reason. Liability claims against the author for material or non-material damages caused by the use or non-use of the information or by the use of incorrect and/or incomplete information are excluded in principle. Therefore, any legal and damage claims are also excluded. This work was compiled and written down with the greatest care and to the best of our knowledge. However, the author accepts no responsibility for the topicality, completeness and quality of the information. Printing errors and misinformation cannot be completely excluded. No legal responsibility or liability of any kind can be assumed for incorrect information provided by the author.

Copyright

Imprint

Printed in Great Britain
by Amazon

CW00468456

A *PetLove* Guide to

The Rottweiler

A *PetLove* Guide to

The Rottweiler

Everything you need to know about your Rottweiler,
including health care, training, breeding and showing

Joan Blackmore

A *PetLove* Guide

© 1987 Salamander Books Ltd.,
129–137 York Way,
London N7 8LG,
United Kingdom.

This revised edition © 1997 Salamander Books Ltd.

Distributed through the pet trade by Interpet Ltd.,
Vincent Lane, Dorking, Surrey RH4 3YX.

Credits

Editor: Tony Hall   Designer: Glynis Edwards
Photographs: Marc Henrie, Tylla Berger (pp 18, 19), Artur Gallas (pp 15, 19), Mary Macphail (pp 21), Sinclair Stammers/Science Photo Lib. (pp 95).
Illustrations: Ray Hutchins
Colour origination: Rodney Howe Ltd
Typesetting: AKM Associates (UK) Ltd, The Old Mill and SX Composing Ltd., Essex.
Printed in China by Leefung Asco Printers Ltd.

Contents

Introduction	10	Breeding the Rottweiler	72
A history of the breed	16	Feeding and care	84
The Rottweiler puppy	22	Showing and	
Training and behaviour	42	competitive training	98
Health problems	64	Glossary/Appendix	114

Foreword

I first met Joan Blackmore over 20 years ago in London, with her Rottweiler, Panzer. I thought then how well Joan had trained him.
A few years later, I went with my husband Friedrich to visit Joan's house. I was impressed with the caring way in which she behaved with her dogs, the way she spoke to them, the way in which she taught them. Her Rottweilers were friendly and loving.
When Joan asked me to write a foreword for this book, I was delighted to do so. With this book, Joan passes on her years of experience with dogs. Whether you are buying your first Rottweiler, or whether you are breeding for the first time, or even if you are an expert, believe me, there is something of interest for everyone. You will feel Joan's unlimited love and understanding for our Rottweilers. This book will help you to train your Rottweiler into a self-confident friend and guard-dog which will look after your house and family.
Joan, thank you for this book.
Tylla Berger
Mrs Berger is the widow of Freidrich Berger, for many years the Chief Breed Warden for Rottweilers in West Germany.

Author

Joan Blackmore has been working with dogs all her life. She owned her first dog – a Bull Terrier – at 11 years of age, and nine years later qualified another Bull Terrier CDX at working trials. Joan bred, showed and trained Bull Terriers until 1963, when she began her long and successful association with Rottweilers. Her first Rottweiler Emil Blackforest (Panzer), under her tutelage, also qualified for the coveted CDX.

Joan is a past-President and currently Chairman of the Rottweiler Club of Great Britain. She is a show judge of international standing and judged Rottweilers at Crufts' in 1982. Joan has imported six German Rottweilers into Britain over the years, including Bulli v.d. Waldequelle. As well as breeding and judging her Rottweilers, Joan is also an extremely successful trainer of dogs for film and television with over 3000 parts credited over the past 23 years.

Veterinary Consultant

Keith Butt, MA, VetMB(Cantab), MRCVS qualified in 1961 at Cambridge University. He runs his own veterinary practice in Kensington, London, and is himself a breeder and owner of many different breeds of pedigree dogs.

US Consultant

Hal Sundstrom, as president of Halamar Inc, publishers, of North Virginia, has been editing and publishing magazines on travel and pure-bred dogs since 1972. He is the recipient of six national writing and public excellence awards from the Dog Writer's Association of America, of which he is now president, and he is a past president of Collie Club of America.

Hal has an extensive background and enormous experience in the dog world as a breeder/handler/exhibitor, match and sweeps judge, officer and director of specialty and all-breed clubs, show and symposium chairman, and officer of the Arizona and Hawaii Councils of Dog Clubs.

Photographer

Marc Henrie began his career as a Stills man at the famous Ealing Film Studios in London. He then moved to Hollywood where he worked for MGM, RKO, Paramount and Warner Brothers.

After he had returned to England, Marc specialized in photographing dogs and cats, establishing an international reputation.

He has won numerous photographic awards, most recently the Kodak Award for the Best Animal Photograph and the Neal Foundation Award for Outstanding Photography of Animal Behaviour.

Marc is married to ex-ballet dancer, Fiona Henrie. They live in West London with their daughter Fleur, two King Charles Cavalier Spaniels and a cat called Topaz.

Author's acknowledgements

The author wishes to thank Annette Colbourne, Violet Slade and Jane and Michael Heath for allowing their dogs to be photographed; Tylla Berger and Artur Gallas of Dortmund for their invaluable help in West Germany; Mary Macphail for her support; all the Blackmore, Murphy and Dean families and last but not least Molly Redman for typing the manuscript.

Introduction

Is the Rottweiler for you?

The Rottweiler is a very interesting and rewarding dog – but only for certain types of human temperament. The powerful frame and equally powerful mind of this breed is not to be taken on without a lot of thought and a real interest in the dog itself.

The males can reach up to 27in (69cm) at the shoulder and can weigh over 125lb (57kg), so with a breed like this you must be sure that you have the dog under control at all times and insist that it uses its mind and strength for you and not against you. A Rottweiler on your side is a wonderful animal, a Rottweiler working against you is the exact opposite.

This breed is also expensive to maintain. They need good quality food and have large appetites, so keep this firmly in mind: be sure that you can afford to feed and house such a large dog, and that you have a suitable, well-fenced garden or yard.

Nervous people looking for a cheap burglar alarm will find it better to consult a firm of security lock specialists, since an untrained Rottweiler can do a lot more damage to your home than the average burglar!

Equally, the young macho male looking for an accessory to his tough image, and encouraging a young Rottweiler to roar at all and sundry, will soon find himself in court and the luckless dog could easily have a destruction order slapped on it.

People looking for a dog to chain in their yard to deter wrongdoers could also find themselves in trouble with a Rottweiler as, unloved and untrained, the dog will at best howl loudly in loneliness and despair and, at worst, bite the person inflicting this terrible suffering!

What type of person should have a Rottweiler?

(a) The owner should be ready to teach the dog all the basic things it needs to know;

(b) should be prepared to make the dog part of the family unit, subject to all the rules imposed by the average family;

(c) must have a sense of fair play, a sense of humour and the ability to make pleasure or displeasure felt very keenly by the dog;

(d) should make sure that all members of the family love, respect and want the dog as much as he or she does, and are prepared to be as firm and fair to the dog as he or she is, with one member of the family at home all day.

Having said all this, the Rottweiler in a good environment is a joy to own; when nothing is happening the Rottweiler sleeps, but when danger threatens the dog is ready and willing to face it. When you want to play, your Rottweiler is eager to join in the game. This breed is not given to senseless barking – when the Rottweiler barks, go and look, as there is usually a good reason. If you like love and cuddles, your macho Rottweiler loves them too, for they have a very soft heart with the family and friends.

Some members of this breed are 'growlers' – that is to say, they grumble in a friendly way when their back is rubbed. It is almost a way of 'talking' their pleasure. Some Rottweilers, on the other hand, hate over-familiarity by strangers, especially the 'all dogs love me' types who grab a dog roughly and slap it about in a supposedly friendly way. If you see your Rottweiler in this situation, step in and tell the offending person to stop. The dog will tell you of his anger by going very still, and a very 'black' expression will come into his eyes. That is the point when, unless the offender stops, the dog will make his dislike of such treatment felt! I must stress that not all Rottweilers do this, but it is as well to

Left: *Rottweilers are happiest when they are included in all aspects of family life.*

Below: *If you can train, feed and house a Rottweiler well, you will have an invaluable companion.*

know that some do, and be warned. It is not easy to tell friends to leave your dog alone, but to own a Rottweiler you have to be as honest and tough as the dogs themselves.

This breed is a working dog and, although they do not make you feel like the world's best dog trainer as do some of the shepherd breeds, once trained they still retain their pride and are very seldom slavish. They are more likely to assume the role of a good mate.

Generally speaking, the Rottweiler loves his home and family and has little desire to stray off. I have only known four Rottweilers who strayed, and they all lived on large country estates with no perimeter visible to them, and all were left to their own devices for hours. With no guidance or 'lines' which must not be crossed, they were unable to recognize the rules.

The Rottweiler in society

Children and Rottweilers get on well, providing the owner is a good referee. Rebuke the child who is misbehaving with the dog, and vice versa: both must learn to respect the other! I only know one Rottweiler who has bitten a child; the dog was provoked by having an ice lolly stick poked into his rectum and he gave the child a nip with jaws that could have broken the child's arm. The dog was subsequently re-homed in a family with three delightful children and he lived happily until he died, with no problems at all.

Left: *In show position, the champion Rottweiler at Crufts' 1987, CH. Aylsham Beauty of Potterspride.*

Above: *Another aspect of owning a Rottweiler is carting; made possible by the breed's strength and will to work.*

If you wish to have your dog accept cats, horses, cattle, sheep and other dogs, you must introduce them from an early age and very sternly rebuke the dog for any chasing or worrying. It is essential that you have the strength of character to insist on perfect behaviour; you will find that you will get acceptance if you demand that your dog conforms to high standards of obedience. A wishy-washy approach will fail to bring out the best in the Rottweiler. This, obviously, applies to all training.

Males of this breed can be very aggressive with other dogs. It is as well to anticipate this, and deal with the dog very firmly the first time he tries it on. There is nothing nicer than a male Rottweiler which has enough self confidence and training to totally ignore other dogs in any situation, and nothing worse than one which wants to bully every other dog. It is up to the owner to make it clear that such behaviour will not be tolerated.

The Rottweiler is a very special dog: a well-trained member of this breed is a constant delight and popular with everyone, whereas the misunderstood, untrained or thoroughly spoilt Rottweiler is a disgrace to the breed at best and, at worst, is a menace and may need to be put down.

Above: *An example of a long-haired Rottweiler. Note the hairy fringing on the ears, chest and back of legs.*

Right: *Blitz, owned and trained by Artur Gallas of Dortmund. This was originally a problem dog before training.*

So remember, a dog is what you make it, by training or environment or upbringing, call it what you will. If you do not have the time or the patience to socialize and teach your dog, then please do not buy a Rottweiler as this is not the breed for you. I see many so-called 'problem dogs' during the course of my work, and 99 per cent of them are simply ill-educated or misunderstood. Once the owners realize why their dog behaves as it does, then one can begin to teach them remedial procedures. Sadly, some owners are just not capable of teaching their dog.

This breed is not for ignorant, unperceptive, non-positive people. Rottweiler owners *must* be able to react in a positive way to be clear in their training methods, to be fun but fair and firm. They need to be hard enough to administer punishment when necessary, in a swift but effective way, but equally quick to praise and love when the dog has behaved correctly. So that he is in no doubt as to what is the right conduct.

14

The results of neglect

Due to the recent increase in demand for these dogs, many Rottweilers are being bred from untypical, un-X-rayed (to check for hip dysplasia) and bad temperamented parents, mainly due to greed or ignorance. Many people are neglectful when they breed a litter, selling pups to just anyone; later on, the pups, in their turn, get bred from, un-X-rayed, often to 'Fred' down the road who is also un-X-rayed but is said to be a 'lovely big dog' as though great size were a breed feature. In fact, oversized Rottweilers usually die earlier, are more prone to lameness for various reasons, and are often too slow to do a good day's work. So, in just a few generations have come litters of potential cripples looking vaguely like real Rottweilers, being sold for a pittance and ending up in dog homes all over the country. I can see no merit at all in the fact that over 5000 Rottweiler puppies were registered in Britain in 1986, or that over 2400 Rottweilers were registered in the USA in December 1986 alone!

If you are thinking of buying a Rottweiler, please re-read this chapter and also carefully consider the next chapter before deciding honestly if this dog is for you. If your decision is 'yes', then I hope that you will choose carefully, rear lavishly, train thoroughly and love mightily, and you will enjoy one of the most rewarding experiences a dog can give.

15

Chapter One

A HISTORY OF THE BREED

The origins
The Rottweiler of legend
The A.D.R.K.

THE ORIGINS

The Rottweiler's origins go back to Roman times. When the mighty legions marched long distances to do battle, they had no refrigerated trucks, or cans of bully beef, so supplies had to be live, on the hoof. Hardy, powerful dogs were needed to control the herds of cattle and a dog very much like the Rottweiler was used; it may not have been the black and tan standard type, but our dogs today carry this tenacious and brave heritage. For those dogs were brave, having to deal with cattle which were probably not as placid as the average milking cow today The herds had to be protected from marauding wolves or even cattle rustlers, the treks were arduous routes across mountains and rivers, heat and intense cold had to be borne with equal fortitude. At the end of the march these dogs would defend their masters in battle with great courage.

In those times, wounds would either get better or the man and his dog would die. There were no drugs, no hospitals, so they had to be tough to survive. Little packs of these dogs would sometimes be left behind, and in the small town of Rottweil, which was once a Roman settlement and is now part of West Germany, they became popular as local cattle-herding dogs. Nestling on the banks of the Neckar River, Rottweil was a market town, to which farmers would bring herds for sale, using their dogs to halve the work.

There is a nice little story which tells of farmers getting drunk on the proceeds of a good day's business, but first tying their bags of gold around the necks of the dogs to ensure the safety of their money. True or false we shall never know, but it has gone down as legend.

When the railroads came and the movement of cattle by road over long distances was banned

Top: *Ralph v. Neckar, 1907 Note the long back and muzzle, the lack of substance; the shoulder and reachy neck.*

Below centre: *Jack v. Schifferstadt. The dog is now showing more substance, with a stronger head and top line.*

by law, the Rottweiler was out of a job. Some people used them to pull carts full of produce, but their main task was denied them. For a time the dogs which had been called Metzgerhunde (butcher's dog) were ignored. Numbers declined, until in 1905 there was only one bitch left in

Bottom left: *Seiglinde v.d. Steinlach. A bitch with a strong head and good top line.*

Above: *Leo v. Cannstatt. Note how the head is improving and good body is coming through.*

Below: *International Champion Hexe v. Marchenwald, 1977. Sister to UK and US champions.*

Rottweil itself, though elsewhere the breed had survived. Matters were improving, however. In 1899 the first breed club was formed under the title: 'The International Club for Leonberger and Rottweiler Dogs'. This unfortunately did not survive for very long and it was not until 1907 that the breed finally got the organization it deserved with the formation of The German Rottweiler Club in Heidelberg. This was the first club to organize Rottweiler breeding systematically. About ten years later in 1910, the breed became recognized as a service dog, capable of police and army duties, and from that time onwards this breed went from strength to strength.

THE ROTTWEILER OF LEGEND

Another story, from the time of Kaiser Wilhelm II, was about a policeman and his Rottweiler in Kiel. The pair were sent off to sort out a fight in a tavern where a large number of drunken sailors were really going to town. The policeman and his dog went in, restored peace, made several arrests and escorted the prisoners back to the jail. Apparently, when the Kaiser

heard about the incident, he expressed a wish to meet the policeman and his police dog. Before the Kaiser could shake the hand of the hero it was required that the policeman remove his helmet to signal to his Rottweiler that he was 'off duty' before anyone could touch him.

The sterling qualities of this breed made it a good war dog, too, especially for patrolling areas where silence was essential. Some breeds get excited, whining and barking when taken out to work; not the Rottweiler, which calmly goes ahead doing the job·with the minimum of fuss and dealing with any wrongdoers in the same strong, efficient way.

I once spoke to a man who was 'taken' by a Rottweiler patrol dog during the last war. The man was desperate to escape and stabbed the dog with a knife, but the dog hung on and though both were bleeding profusely, it would not let him go until the handler came and called 'Aus' (out), whereupon the dog released his grip and let the handler arrest the man.

I actually saw the scars on the arm of the man telling the story; it must have been horrific to have experienced that incident, but the strangest thing of all was that sitting at my storyteller's feet was a large male Rottweiler. He bought a Rottweiler years later because he was so impressed with the dog which arrested him, which changed from a ferocious foe one minute to a calm, trained dog the next: even though the dog was badly wounded he never forgot to obey his handler instantly.

THE A.D.R.K.

In the early 1920s the A.D.R.K. (Allgemeiner Deutscher Rottweiler Klub – General German Rottweiler Club) was formed. The A.D.R.K. do much to ensure that the Rottweiler remains correct in mind, heart, health and conformation: a rigid code of conduct for both breeders and owners is maintained, with X-rays for hip dysplasia, hard working trials, tests of suitability for breeding and a great deal more insistence on breeding only from the best than most Kennel Clubs display.

I think it is time the strict A.D.R.K. rules were applied worldwide. If people had to prove good hips by X-ray results, and demonstrate their dogs' bravery, ability to work and good conformation, then we would ensure that the Rottweiler never degenerates into a black and tan

Above: *Rintelna the Bombadier CDEX UDEX, sire of the author's first Rottweiler, Panzer.*

travesty of what once was the best in the world.

It is up to all of us now to make sure that our grandchildren and their children find the Rottweiler as good as they were in days gone by – not 'improved' by exaggerated breed points, but free from painful inherited diseases, sound in mind, retaining that essential inner character of calmness, bravery and ability to work and still looking like real Rottweilers, strong, sound and true.

Let me give you a wonderful quotation by the Countess Aga von Hagen who described the breed in her book published in 1955. "He makes a clear distinction between 'on duty' and 'off duty'. The ferocious guardian becomes a lamb in private life. There is nothing foppish about the Rottweiler. His noble qualities are those of strength, cheerfulness and a warm heart." These lines sum up the traits that typify this breed.

Chapter Two

THE ROTTWEILER PUPPY

Choosing a puppy
Conformation
Checking for problems
Coming home
Crime and punishment
Diet
Socialization
House and garden

CHOOSING A PUPPY AND THE FIRST SIX MONTHS

Having decided that you would like to own a Rottweiler, how do you select the person from whom you will purchase the puppy?

There are weekly dog papers published in most countries which contain advertisements from breeders, and there are also Rottweiler Clubs where information on the breed and lists of breeders can be obtained. The addresses of most clubs can be had from the Kennel Club or the leading official canine body for all breeds. (Some addresses are at the back of this book).

It is essential that you select your breeder wisely, so what do you look for when you visit to discuss the possibility of your buying a puppy?

(a) Check that the breeder is checking you out too: are they asking relevant questions and doing their best to ensure that you are suitable for a Rottweiler?

(b) Are they prepared to show you their official hip dysplasia results of the parents and other related dogs?

(c) Do they have a good after-sales help and advice service should you need guidance from them on rearing and training problems when the pup is growing up?

(d) How do their own dogs behave? Are they obedient, sensible and the kind of dog you want to own?

Above: *A litter of puppies is an irresistible sight, but ask the right questions before buying.*

Below: *An example of a well-designed kennel area, with fire equipment easily to hand.*

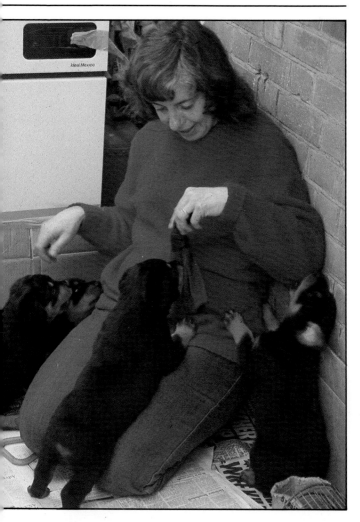

(e) The general impression: are the dogs from this kennel well-housed, well-fed, happy and confident? Does the breeder take a real interest in you and your needs and inspire confidence in you? Do you feel that he or she has the ability to help and advise you?

If the answer to all these questions is 'yes', then go ahead and look at the pups (provided, of course, that the breeder is happy with you too). When you look at Rottweiler puppies you cannot always go by the old rule of choosing the one which

Above: *Playtime can be used to form a close relationship with your puppy and to begin to teach it some simple words.*

comes to you, since most Rottweiler pups will rush at you for a fuss – eating your shoelaces and chewing your trouser bottoms!

CONFORMATION

If you are looking for a pup to show later on, select one which conforms as closely as possible

Above: *Check for a scissor bite, where the top teeth fit snugly over the lower ones at the front.*

to the breed standard (see p.100). Look for a broad head with a good stop, neat, high-set ears, dark almond-shaped eyes, and a scissor bite (top teeth fitting neatly over the lower ones at the front).

The body should look neither over-long nor too short, and there should be a big roomy rib cage with strong straight front legs, the feet turning neither in nor out. They should be well knuckled, not spread or flat. The back should be straight, and the part close to the tail (the croup) should not fall away as it does in, for example, the German Shepherd.

The puppy should be viewed from the rear; the hind legs should not be cow hocked. Watch the puppy move about; is it jaunty and true in movement? An experienced dog person will feel for the skeletal structure, ie, the lay of the shoulder, but if you are a novice, look at the pup sideways on; does the neck flow into the body or does it look stuck on as an afterthought?

A pup with a well-laid shoulder will appear to flow nicely

Right: *Look at the puppy from the rear to make sure it does not have cow hocks (when the hind legs bend inwards as shown).*

26

together, neck with body, and a pup with good shoulders usually has a nicely angulated rear too.

Do not look for over-angulation in Rottweilers, but you do not want back legs which are dead straight, thin and lacking in power. The back end is the 'motor'; it provides the propulsion. If you do not have a good back end you do not have much of a working dog.

Overall, is the pup pleasing to the eye? Remember, if you want a pup to show, you should know your breed standard by heart and perhaps have attended a few shows to 'get your eye in'.

For the person choosing a pup to work, I would pick one with panache that is full of itself. My own preference for a working dog is to pick a slightly longer backed pup, as they seem to

Above: *Check the puppy all over for any signs of lice, which look like grains of sand, and fleas.*

have more ease with jumps and agility later on. I would also like to see if the parents work well too, as I am sure the desire to work is inherited.

The vast majority of people are looking for a companion guard, so they are not interested in breeding, working or showing and can therefore accept minor faults. A pup with a few white hairs on the chest will be just as good a dog to live with as one without, and you probably would not even notice if your pup had a lighter eye than is desirable. I even find that some people actually ask for, and are prepared to await, a long-coated

27

Rottweiler. They are very handsome, but taboo for breeding or showing. You can expect to pay a little less for a dog which is not up to show standard; some breeders only give a pedigree and no registration with a pet puppy. It is a good idea, since it does stop indiscriminate breeding.

However, if you think that you may like to have a litter later on, then please pick a really good pup and pay the correct price. Do not forget that we all want to improve the breed and not see it deteriorate: the Rottweiler is in trouble enough from people breeding from poor stock.

CHECKING FOR PROBLEMS

Check the puppy for fleas, lice or other parasites. Lice look like grains of sand and feel like little scabs. Fleas are hard to see in black coats, but look out for gritty black bits or the fleas themselves. The ears should be clean, with no sign of ear mites (brown, greasy secretions in the ears). Examine the eyes, look for signs of inturning eyelids (a condition called entropion, which causes great distress and usually means surgery later on).

The front dew claws can be left on but the back ones should have been removed.

Look at the puppy's stomach: it

Below: *While you are examining the puppy look inside the ears for ear mites.*

Bottom: *Look for a broad head with a good stop. Ears should be neat and high-set, eyes almond-shaped and dark.*

Above: *Examine the puppy's stomach to see that there is no genital discharge or hernia.*

should be clean and free from rashes or pimples, and there should be no discharge from the genital areas. Male puppies should be gently felt to ensure that two testicles are present; in a very young pup they may not be easy to find! Look at the 'belly button' area; a lump there means a hernia. Some disappear as the pup grows, but some may need surgery. Ask when the pup was wormed, and the name of the product used – your puppy could be afflicted later and you may need to worm again.

COMING HOME

Your breeder should supply you with a diet sheet and some may even give you a supply of the feed to which your pup has been used, in order that it will not get loose motions from a change of diet, home, and the general trauma of the move.

The first night is usually noisy. Give the pup a warm place to sleep with a cardboard box (*not a stapled one*) for a bed, as it is cheap, draughtproof and not dangerous if chewed. Do not go and comfort the pup during the night, or it will howl for you to come again. Do not let the pup sleep on your bed – it may seem a good idea at eight weeks, but in a year's time 100 lb (45kg) plus of Rottweiler on your bed will give you bad leg cramps.

My personal preference is for a puppy to be reared in the house if it is to achieve its full potential as an adult: just living with you on an every day basis teaches the pup so many things. Without even realizing it, when your puppy is with you all the time you are teaching it the rules of life.

Should you wish to have a kennel and run outside for later on, it must be well constructed and lined, as any projecting edge will be chewed! A wooden floor raised from the ground is best, as it is warmer than concrete, and there should be a strong chew-proof bed. Metal – that is, aluminium angle section – can be used on the edges of the box. Sawdust on the floor is my choice, but you can use newspaper if you wish, though I find it goes soggy and disintegrates easily, making cleaning out a messy business.

The run can be concrete, or a concrete perimeter path with a shingle area inside. You will need to dig out to a depth of about 12 inches (30cm) and fill with shingle; this is easy to clean and disinfect. Some people use paving slabs, but when excrement gets between the cracks it is not very hygienic. Drainage is important; the water must have somewhere to go when you hose out your run, so think of that aspect too.

It is essential that the puppy in the house has access to an outside area for the purpose of toilet training and for playing in the fresh air and sunshine – two vital things. There is nothing like getting a bit of sun on their backs for raising healthy puppies.

It is important that you play with your puppy. There are all kinds of dog toys on the market, or you can make your own from the leg of an old pair of jeans with a knot in it. This makes a lovely tugging toy, which you can use for throwing and playing tug-of-war, as it is strong, cheap and cannot harm your pup. If you can obtain a block of hardwood, this makes a good chew toy, as it

doesn't disintegrate. We found an old hardwood cylinder which was once used as a roller in a machine. It has survived 11 generations of pups and is still going strong.

Never give your puppy an old slipper or shoe, since old shoes look and smell just like new ones, with the inevitable consequences. Never use tennis-sized balls with adult Rottweilers, as these can become lodged at the back of the throat and suffocate your dog – always buy the extra-large solid rubber dog balls, which are much safer. Our adults love to play with old tyres – we roped one to an old apple tree and it is very popular to grab and swing on. They like to play with tyres on the ground too.

When the puppy is sleeping, it must be allowed to relax in peace. The children must be taught that the puppy's bed is sacred, and never to disturb a pup sleeping; then, when the pup

Below: *A tug-of-war can be fun for both you and the puppy. Make sure the puppy 'gives' the object when the game is over.*

has had enough of playing, it knows that its bed is a safe sanctuary.

When visitors come, do not let them encourage your puppy to chew at their clothes; a firm 'No', accompanied by a sharp slap, will stop most pups. It is not a

Below: *A block of hardwood, a dog ball, the leg of an old pair of jeans and a bone are safe toys.*

Bottom: *An old tyre can provide hours of great amusement as well as healthy exercise.*

good idea to let your puppy use you or your visitors as a biting toy. Most men, for some reason, like to play rough wrestling games with puppies. I do not think this is a good idea as, if you let the pup win, it could get the idea that you can be beaten – not a good attitude at all for a pup to adopt – or, if you win all the time, you diminish the pup's self confidence and could even damage it physically. It is much better to play tug-of-war, throwing and fetching games, etc, as these aid training and are just as much fun.

CRIME AND PUNISHMENT

If you need to rebuke a young pup, shake it quite hard by the scruff of the neck and use a very angry voice – just the way the mother would rebuke a pup. If you could see how hard a good mother checks her pups you would not worry about being too tough. Should your puppy decide to retaliate, repeat the rebuke even harder till the pup squeals, then instantly let go and return to normal. The rules are: if you need to punish, it must be the instant the pup is doing the bad deed; it must be strong, accompanied by an angry voice; and forgiveness must be just as swift – never, never nag!

When you feed your puppy, you *must* teach it to allow you to remove the dish or touch it when it is feeding – there is nothing worse than an adult Rottweiler

Below: *Teach your puppy at an early stage that it must allow its dinner bowl to be removed.*

Bottom: *Max 'gives' his bone. Always ensure adults are present when children are handling dogs.*

which is possessive over food, bones or toys. Start while it is young; give your pup its dish of food, then sometimes put a few extra bits in by hand and other times take the dish, so that your pup accepts your will at all times and learns that your hand coming in may mean that it gets extra goodies. If your pup growls, rebuke it, with a slap or a shake – telling it what a very good puppy it is when it stops growling, and adding a few tasty morsels by hand to the bowl.

The same applies to toys. Teach your pup to 'give' or 'leave' when it has a toy, with much praise when it does and a little game as a special reward. Praise and Punishment are key words,

Above: *The leg of an old pair of jeans, tied in a knot, is a good toy for a tugging game.*

but always be fair and never, ever punish in temper; you will go over the top and that is never a good thing. If you need to punish, make it swift. One hard slap and a really angry voice followed by instant forgiveness is much better than silly little slaps, nagging or, worse, a severe beating.

It should never be necessary to beat any dog severely if it is raised correctly. I very seldom have even to slap my own dogs because they fear my angry voice, and they know that I will punish them if I have to – so usually I do not have to, since they all have respect and love for me. The fear of what I might be able to do is greater than actually knowing my limitations! Beating severely only shows the dog the extent of punishment and may even harden the dog. Rottweilers do not care too much about physical pain, but you can break their hearts easily once they give you all their love and trust. It is better to do things the easy way and gain their love and respect from puppyhood.

You can actually teach your dog to bite you if you punish him by thrashing. Think about it: if the pain is so severe, he will almost *have* to bite you out of self preservation to make you stop. So remember always: one hard slap is better than a beating. Do it from puppyhood and you will end up with a dog on which you only need to use verbal rebukes.

Try always to get into the mind of your dog. Think about life from

Below: *Your dog should wait when the door is opened. Rushing ahead is dangerous.*

the puppy's point of view, bearing in mind that the puppy's mind is simple and not in any way capable of human reasoning; but if you, instead, can 'think like a dog', you will be a little more understanding.

A dog is a pack animal, and it needs its human to be a good 'pack leader'. It should be shown the rules in a simple way: no dog pack leader would allow a member of the pack to cheek him, precede him through a door

or give him any aggravation at all. The offender would be quickly bowled over and bitten hard to remind it of its place.

We ask dogs to live by our laws but we must try to understand a little of their ancestral laws too. Dogs are still possessed of their primitive instincts. For example, if a member of the pack is injured and yelping, the pack will kill it; survival of the fittest is the rule. It sounds harsh to us, but it is a kinder way than leaving an

Above: *The dog is a pack animal and as such still obeys primitive laws of dominance and survival within the group it inhabits.*

injured member to die slowly over several days. Circling to make a bed is on a par with trampling down the grass in the wild. Bone burying is to preserve food and the constant urination of males is to mark territory: it is all part of their inborn heritage.

DIET

Your breeder will have given you a diet sheet which you should try to stick to as far as possible. There are dozens of ways to feed a dog well, but remember it needs to have a well-balanced diet. Shown below is my own simple diet sheet which has been tried and tested over a period of 25 years or so:

First meal: All in one meal, well soaked with puppy milk.

Second meal: All in one meal, soaked with cooked mince, fish or hard-boiled eggs.

Third meal: As first.

Fourth meal: As second.

Three months: Three meals daily.

Six months: Two meals daily.
One year: One meal daily.

Don't fall into the trap of overdosing your pup with vitamins – only use a vitamin supplement if you are feeding a fresh meat and wholemeal biscuit diet which is not supplemented already. Most manufactured dog foods contain supplements of vitamins, minerals and trace elements, so if you add more you will unbalance the formula and cause all kinds of problems since it is more dangerous to over vitaminize than to under vitaminize. A tiny drop of cod liver oil is beneficial to older dogs, but don't overdo it as too much causes disorders.

A growing Rottweiler needs a diet consisting of about half protein and half carbohydrate. Many people use the all-in-one feeds and, as they are fairly high in protein, you only need to add a little extra protein for a balanced diet if this is what you are feeding. These products are also vitaminized, so you do not need to use supplements. Always read the ingredients on the pack.

If you use milk powder, make sure it is a brand name product, as some pet shops sell calf weaner in plain bags as puppy milk, and this will scour the pup very badly (that is, cause diarrhoea).

Many people worry over the quantity of each meal. I stick to the method my father used with his Bull Terriers – approximately the size of the pup's head per meal – and this works well. With an eight-week old pup on four meals a day, the head is small; then, when the pup is twelve weeks and going on to three meals daily, the head is larger so the meals get larger too. Simple but effective!

Do not forget to leave fresh water available at all times in a heavy bowl. Pups love to pick up water bowls for some reason and the floor gets very wet. However, an earthenware bowl is slippery to pick up, heavy, and not so much fun as a plastic or steel bowl.

Keep your puppy lean, not fat, if you want your adult Rottweiler to be free of hip dysplasia. Young bones should not have to carry excess poundage if they are to grow straight and true, so no choc-drops, pieces of cake or other rubbish! Do not fatten your puppy in order to win puppy classes; it is far better to keep the pup lean and win Open Classes later on with a dog which has good hips. I have been appalled when judging puppy classes to see the waddling puddings in the ring and make a point of telling the owners off after the judging.

Top right: *A large juicy bone will invariably be a favourite toy, guaranteed to keep any dog engrossed for ages.*

Right: *Puppies must not be overfed. Remember that overfeeding and too many vitamins can lead to bad hips and poor health. Puppies must always be kept lean.*

SOCIALIZATION

Socialization is an important aspect of puppy rearing. Take your pup out in the car from day one. *Do not* take him out of the car as he will not have had all his inoculations, but just drive around the block so that the pup does not grow up to be travel sick. Visit friends with the pup and give it as much socialization as possible.

After the pup has had its final inoculations and been blood-tested for parvo virus levels, then the real work can begin. Take the pup to the school to collect the children, visit your local pub or bar with it, and walk a little way down the high street so the pup sees traffic, people and other paraphernalia of modern life. It is not a bad idea at this stage to take out some veterinary and third party insurance – it could save you money later on.

Enrol at your local training class and do about ten minutes in the park daily with the pup off the lead, so that it can meet other dogs. Do not let the pup rampage around too much in play, as they are easily damaged at this age, and do not overdo the exercise; ten minutes is enough at first. It is dangerous to over-exercise a young Rottweiler because they need all their calories to be used in growing rather than in too much exercise and, most important, too much wear and tear on soft, growing bones can cause damage to the skeletal structure. In the garden at home the pup will play and then flop down to sleep. That is good, natural exercise, with the

Below: *A puppy must be socialized so that it will learn not to harass other animals.*

chance to rest when need be.

Many people ask when to use a check chain on the pup. I like to use a light leather puppy collar until the pup is used to the lead and I never use a check chain until the pup is leaning into the collar and is happy enough with the feel of it to pull ahead. There is no rule as every pup is an individual, but generally I do not use a check chain until about six months and then it is essential to use it correctly (see p.55).

If you have another dog or cat in your home when the new pup arrives, you must allow the older dog to growl at the pup if it torments; do not expect the established dog to take to the pup instantly. Pups are a pest to older dogs at first, with their needle teeth and playful ways. Let the older dog chastise the pup when need be while you act as a good referee. Tell the dog that he is still number one and make a great fuss of him too, and you will find that they will become friends.

Your cat will probably feel like

Above: *A well-trained dog and cat can live together in perfect harmony. teach you puppy at once that it is not acceptable behaviour to torment the cat.*

leaving home when a pup arrives, so you must let your little Rottweiler know from the first that it must not harry the cat, and in a week there will be peace.

It is not clever to teach your dog to chase cats as there could come a day when your dog chases a cat across the road and is killed; anyway, the cat could be some child's much loved pet!

I hope that you checked all your garden fences for gaps before the puppy arrived – your neighbours will not love you if the puppy gets into their garden and eats their flowers. It is important to keep in with your neighbours when you have a dog; if it is a nuisance to them it is not unknown for a piece of poisoned meat to be flung over the fence. As usual, it is the dog who suffers.

HOUSE AND GARDEN

It is very useful to have some sort of playpen where the puppy can be popped when necessary. We all have days when the phone is ringing, the children are yelling and the pup is being a pest, and it is far better to put the pup in the playpen for an hour than end up getting angry with everyone. At first the pup may yelp to come out, but it is important that you teach it to remain where you wish it to be, so persevere. Obviously, you should not leave the pup in a pen for too long or it will begin to hate the area. Make sure that it has toys and perhaps a few large dog biscuits to chew on, and never take the pup out till it has stopped yelling! Do not give in – your dog must never beat you at anything.

Be careful about shoving young children and puppies unsupervised into the garden just for a bit of peace – my young niece, aged three, was once caught bouncing an eight-week old pup on its head by the back legs! Little children do not realize that they can be very cruel so please, *always* supervise.

Some pups pick up stones, plastic toys and other rubbish, which they swallow. This can cause a blockage, in which case the pup will be listless, off its food and either not passing motions or getting very liquid motions. At any sign of being off-colour you should call your veterinary surgeon; if you know that your pup is a picker-up of such rubbish, tell the vet so that he will know all the facts.

When you leave your puppy for any period, try to look around the room and remove any items which look chewable, for example shoes, children's toys,

Below: *Newspaper makes a warm bed. Change it frequently or it will disintegrate, making a mess.*

etc. Electric flex should have a barricade of some sort so that you don't get a fried puppy. Dangling tea towels are fair game and knobs which stick out just have to be tasted. I once heard of a method for anti-pup chew paste, consisting of chilli peppers, the hottest available, boiled in oil until they formed a paste which could be painted on to areas which get chewed. Mustard is good, too, but some very naughty pups seem to think it adds flavour!

Bitter aloes is another herb which is also said to work well, although I think that it is better to give the pup a distraction. Take a marrow bone, remove the knobby ends with a hacksaw, push out the marrow and push a bit of cooked meat right into the middle of the bone so the pup cannot reach it; they spend hours trying to get it out and ignore the rest of the room.

> So, let us re-cap a little:
> (a) *Don't* have a fat puppy
> (b) *Don't* over-exercise
> (c) *Do* socialize
> (d) When you need to rebuke, use a hard slap or shake accompanied by a very angry tone; a rebuke must be swift, hard and over quickly, with instant forgiveness
> (e) Praise must be lavish – combine fun with firmness

One final word: do not encourage your pup to be aggressive. They guard quite naturally from about 18 months onwards and if you try to 'sharpen up' the pup, you may well end up holding a tiger by the tail. Rottweilers do not need egging on; they do the job of protecting quite naturally.

Below: *Outdoor games in the fresh air and sunshine are the best thing for growing puppies.*

Chapter Three

TRAINING AND BEHAVIOUR

Training problems
Training routines
'No!'
Supremacy
Retrieving
Communication
Aggression
Stealing
Advanced training

TRAINING PROBLEMS

You should start to train your Rottweiler as soon as you get it – puppy training is a steady on-going procedure. Begin with house training, ie, where and where not the pup can relieve itself. Leave lots of newspapers by the back door for the pup to use as a toilet, depending on the age of the pup. They cannot usually wait all night until at least 12 weeks. Vigilance is the key word with house training: put the pup out of doors after every meal and watch for signs of sniffing and circling – this means that it needs to 'go'.

Praise like mad for all toilets done outside. Some people manage to make their pups think that the act of going to the toilet at all is bad, thus making their dogs 'secret piddlers': they feel the need to piddle, or worse, only when they cannot be seen by humans – not nice when you find wet patches behind the sofa!

It must be made clear that certain places, ie outside, are good, and inside is bad. The crate system is a good one; using the principle that a dog hates to soil his sleeping place, it is popped into a large wire crate last thing at night and let out in the morning into the garden. You must, of course, accustom the dog to the crate gradually for short periods during the day so that it becomes a comfortable place and not a punishment. Try feeding the pup in the crate so that it associates it with pleasure. Never leave the pup for hours in the crate during the day – a little and often is the rule.

Most puppies will come to a pleasant calling sound as they associate this with the arrival of food. I always yell, 'Puppies come,' when I go to the paddock to feed them. Whatever wonderful game is being played will cease as soon as they hear that call, and they come flying for their food. Thus I have begun to teach them what 'come' means. Sometimes I just go out and call 'Puppies come' when I want to play with them. It has the same effect; they rush up for a romp and a cuddle, and I am establishing a reward for 'coming' – food, play or affection.

BEGINNING TRAINING ROUTINES

When the puppies leave the litter and enter the house to begin the real business of learning, then you, as the owner, have to learn too. Try to do little things each day. For example, even a tiny eight-week-old pup can learn to 'speak'. Wait till just before feed time and show the pup a tasty morsel. It will try to jump up for it, but stare into the pup's eyes and say, quickly and excitedly,

'Speak.' I have had the most amazing results at this age, but it is essential to convey excitement and give the morsel instantly the pup makes a noise. You must do this exercise with no distractions, as a pup cannot concentrate for long. Try to pick a time when nobody is liable to enter the room or move suddenly, as once the pup's eyes leave yours, you have broken the spell. 'Speak' is a handy command, as your dog can use it to convey his needs. Mine will 'speak' to the tap over the sink when thirsty, 'speak' at the door when they need to go to the toilet, or sometimes 'speak' to me, when I have to decipher whether it is 'out', 'water', 'play with me', or 'something's wrong'.

It is useful, too, when you get a caller whom you distrust, to hold the dog by the collar and command 'Speak'. Nobody wants to argue with a Rottweiler under those circumstances and trouble just seems to melt away.

Communication is a good thing between you and your dog, and if it knows 'speak' it can draw your attention to so many things. There is no need to worry that your Rottweiler will bark all day; it is just not in their nature and

Below left: *Rottweilers are highly intelligent dogs and can swiftly acquire the knack of dealing with their needs about the house. Here, 'Max' opens the door.*

Below: *'Max' effects an entry to the kitchen. It is useful to train your dog to 'speak' to be let out, to ask for water and to communicate other needs.*

they use their voice only when the need arises.

ESTABLISHING SUPREMACY

With a tough breed such as this you have to constantly remind it of your supremacy. One way is to teach your pup to 'back' when you open a door, making the pup take a few steps back and not scrabble at the door as soon as you move to open it. Every time you open the door, put your foot against the pup's chest and push it, saying, 'Back.' If the pup ignores you, push it a little more roughly and give your voice an angry edge. The reasons for teaching this simple lesson are:

(a) It shows your dog that you are in charge
(b) It stops your dog rushing into possible danger
(c) When the dog is adult and you open the door to the postman or the paper boy, who may have a hand raised to deliver a letter or paper, your dog is under control just behind you ready to defend you – but in the 'stay' position until you give the next command. If the caller is peaceful and legitimate, you know that your well-trained dog will not rush out and bite him.
(d) Dogs which fight to get out of the door before their owner are a nuisance and, if you live by a busy road, they could easily be

killed. You could also have a bill for several thousands of pounds for damages your dog did to the car – so teach this easy lesson.

The same applies to the car. The dog must learn to 'stay' until you say it may enter or leave it – this is a life-saving lesson. If your dog leaps from the car on to a busy road, the consequences could be awful.

Let us talk about teaching the 'stay'. Little pups can learn to do

Below: *Your dog must learn to 'stay' in the car until you give the command to leave it. Leaping from the car on to a busy road may have fatal consequences.*

Above: *If your dog knows how to open the door make sure it knows how to close it as well.*

'baby stays' for a few seconds, increasing weekly. Adults should know already what 'stay' means. Methods are varied, but the easiest is as follows.

Put your dog on a lead, which must be long and preferably leather (see p.60), place the dog in the 'sit' position and give a firm command 'Stay', accompanied by a hand signal (see illustrations). Take a step back from your dog, making sure the lead is slack! The first time you do it your dog will probably move, so make a scolding noise (I use a growly 'Aaargh' sound, but you can say 'No' if you like) and put the dog back in the exact position it was in before. Persist until the dog stays for five seconds, then step back to it, count to three in your head, and praise the dog effusively. Do not do too much at first, but do not give in until you are successful. Ten minutes is ample.

Why count to three when you return to your dog? It teaches the dog to wait until it is released from the command; you do not want the dog leaping all over you when you return to it. I use a special word which tells my dogs the exercise is over. I say 'OK.' This means the dog is no longer doing the exercise and can relax.

One very important thing is the way in which you say the word 'stay'. It should convey to the dog, 'You have no choice, you *have* to do it.' So many people

say 'stay' in the sort of voice that says 'oh, please do it, dear.' It must be a command, not an entreaty.

Do you see how every little step has a reason? For the short daily time you spend teaching your dog civilized behaviour in the first year you will be

Above: *When your dog has learnt to 'stay' step backwards, going a little further each time.*

Below: *Release the dog from the 'stay' position by giving the command to 'come'.*

rewarded with ten or more years with a dog which will be a pleasure and pride to own. When it knows the rules they are there for life.

Once your dog is doing 'stay' on the lead steadily, and clearly knows what you mean, then drop your lead and go further back from it. The next step is to remove the lead and do the exercise. Gradually increase the length of time until your dog will stay for about ten minutes.

Do each exercise step by step; do not be afraid to go back to square one if you need to. In training it is best to progress slowly, and ensure the dog learns each step well. You can eventually go out of sight and know that your dog will stay. One warning; don't do what my husband did. He left his Rottweiler bitch at the 'down stay', became engrossed and forgot her for three hours. She stayed, but he felt terrible! Always release the dog once the exercise is over. Dogs are not robots, so please be fair to them.

Below: *Your dog should learn to 'sit' when he reaches you to complete the exercise.*

'NO!'

You also need a word which tells your puppy that it is doing something bad. 'No' is the most common word, or 'leave' if the puppy is about to chew the carpet or rake out the rubbish bin. Whichever word you use, don't keep changing it; make it easy for a tiny mind to understand. Should your pup ignore the word, either you are being verbally too soft, or you have a pretty dominant pup. Try a second command in a much fiercer tone. If the pup ignores you again, either go up and give it a hard shake by the scruff of the neck, accompanied by an even stronger 'no' or throw an object at the pup. Some Rottweiler pups will try to bite you when corrected, so you must win. Never let a pup get away with aggression towards you; you must give it a very hard slap to establish your authority. Don't forget to make friends again the minute the pup submits. Your total attitude should convey your supremacy to the pup.

It is noticeable how people with natural authority with dogs seldom need to use force.

Somehow the dog just knows that there is a person with whom they will never get away with nonsense. Try to cultivate this frame of mind and it works wonders. Your tone of voice is of prime importance: you must be able to sound totally venomous and, seconds later, you may need to use a voice absolutely dripping with honey. A simple 'Good dog' is not always enough – make your praise lavish and your punishing voice frightening.

I have a magic word: it is 'Right'. This means 'You have gone too far and I am now really angry'. It must be rapped out in a sharp, threatening way – it terrifies my dogs and even works on those I work with which have been trained in other languages. If said in the correct way the word conveys such menace that the message gets through.

MORE COMMANDS

It is also necessary to teach your dog to lie flat. You should use a command and hand signal. Point to the floor, say a firm, decisive 'Down', push the pup behind the shoulders and down he goes. You can also pull out the front legs from a sitting position, or roll him over with a push on the shoulder sideways on. There are harsher methods for older dogs, but you should not need to use them on a pup. Do a little exercise for a few minutes in this command, say five or six times a day, with lots of praise, and within a week your pup will know what 'down' means.

Then you can do 'down stay' for ten seconds, slowly building up to ten minutes. Never forget that pups lack concentration, so do not push on too quickly, and always have a little game after training as a reward.

At about three to four months your pup will start to become more independent and will sometimes refuse to come. Always use the dog's name, for example, 'Rex, come', not just 'Rex', which tells it its name but not what to do. If there is no response, your next move is to pick up an object (a plastic bowl is good) and toss it so that it hits the pup. The impact should be accompanied by 'Rex, come', followed instantly by 'Good dog' when it takes a step towards you and more praise as it continues to come. The pup soon learns that no matter where it is you can

Below: *'Down stay', where the dog lies down rather than sitting, is another useful command.*

make something bad happen to it if it chooses to disobey.

With an older dog, you can throw something harder. A heavy check chain is good, but it must be thrown strongly enough to hurt or the exercise is useless.

Never, never hit a dog when it comes, no matter how angry you are, or you will finish with a dog which is afraid to come to you.

There are people who do not believe in being hard on a dog. That's fine, but such people should never buy a Rottweiler as the breed needs a very firm hand, sometimes on the rump, pretty sharply!

Jumping up is another thing which the pup needs to know about. You need to start teaching the words 'off' or 'get off' from day one. Little muddy paw prints on the fridge door, or your

Above: *Jumping up on command is acceptable; uncontrolled, however, it can be a menace.*

friend's best suit, are not endearing things, so teach your pup by using the word accompanied by a tug on the puppy collar: you should also ask all visitors to help you by using the same word. Don't ever say, 'Oh, it's OK for you to jump up on Fred as he is wearing old jeans, but you can't jump on Auntie Maud,' as that is too confusing for it. The pup either can jump up or it cannot.

It is not a good idea to let pups go up and down stairs as it has a bad effect on bone structure and could be damaging, so when little Rex puts his paws on the stairs say 'Get off.'

RETRIEVING

Teething is a time when a puppy's gums hurt and it needs to chew hard objects, so give it suitable things. Playing tug-of-war with the leg of an old pair of jeans is a good game and helps to pull out the baby teeth. There is a school of thought which says that such games make teeth go undershot but, speaking from experience, I have not found it to be so. It's good fun, a lovely reward game and you can start your retrieve this way too.

Play tug-of-war, then throw the cloth into a corner; your pup will rush to get it and bring it back for another game. If the pup runs off with the cloth, put yourself in a position in the room where you can intercept the pup next time you throw it and take the cloth away. Soon the dog will realize that by bringing the cloth to you the game gets even better. Don't forget to give the command 'Fetch' when you throw the cloth, and within weeks your pup will know another word.

When you give the cloth to the pup, say 'Hold it'. When the pup takes it, praise highly. If you do this every time you give the pup a toy, it will soon know the words 'hold it' – another step on your

way to a good retriever. One tip – always finish a retrieve game while the pup is still keen to do it. Never go on until the pup gets fed up, or you will undo all your good work. If you use a retrieve article, such as a dumb-bell, two retrieves are enough, then put the dumb-bell in a place where the pup can see it, but cannot reach it. You can then talk to the pup about it from time to time, saying things like 'There's your lovely 'fetch' ', and making the pup really want the article.

COMMUNICATION

Talking to your dog is very necessary; not just commands, but normal chat. It is probably seen to be a sign of madness by some people, but then they do not get as much enjoyment and co-operation from their dogs as those who do talk to them. It is important to have a good relationship with your dog – you must understand each other's needs and ways, and talking to the dog is companionable and sociable. You would be surprised

Below: *Early games with your puppy can lead quite easily to training for the retrieve. Good fun for you and your dog.*

Above: *Don't be dissuaded from introducing your dog to other animals. It is always of help.*

at how many words a dog can pick out of a sentence and understand, especially if you speak in a voice which is not a dull monotone. Most dogs know the words 'walk', 'going out' and 'do you want'; they soon learn 'dinner' or 'water' from just listening and association of ideas.

You will notice how quickly a dog learns how certain actions performed by the human in its life affect it. Going to the cupboard where the dog food is kept at certain times means that dinner is coming, putting on certain clothes means that it might be time for a walk, or other clothes mean that it is definitely not time for a walk.

Some Rottweilers have a great sense of humour and will use their mind in a quite uncanny way. For example, a friend of

mine is a cab driver and when he is going to work he always puts on a particular pair of shoes. His Rottweiler noticed this and, sneakily, began to hide just one of the shoes every day, resulting in a frantic half hour search to find the shoe: the dog did not like his owner leaving him, and tried in his simple way to stop it happening. Some scientists do not believe that a dog is capable of such simple reasoning power, but there is a wealth of difference between a laboratory animal and a socialized trained dog, which is taught to use its mind.

As I have said before, if you keep a Rottweiler outside in a kennel it will never develop its full potential as a house pet does. Certainly it is hard work to teach a pup, but look at the rewards – and anyway, it should be good fun too. Training should be enjoyable for you and the dog. There is nothing like the feeling of elation you get when the dog finally understands and performs the action want.

53

CHECKING AGGRESSION

For those of you who already have a Rottweiler, fully grown and perhaps giving you some trouble, here are some of the main problems and a few tips on how to deal with them.

Aggression over food should, of course, have been dealt with in babyhood, but if it wasn't, your dog may be growling over food, bones or possessions. It is always better not to have a stand-up fight with a fully grown Rottweiler unless you are sure you can win! Therefore, you have to beat it with craftiness.

Tie a piece of string round the food bowl with a long length to your hand, get an empty washing-up-liquid bottle and fill it with very cold water (or, in the case of very bad dogs, you can use a small saucepan full of icy water). Put down the bowl and, when the dog begins to eat, say 'Leave'. The dog will not obey you and may growl ominously. Say again, in a very firm voice, 'Rex, leave,' and give the dog a squirt in the face from the bottle, or a good slosh from the saucepan of water. This will usually cause the dog to stop eating in surprise. Then, with a quick tug, pull the bowl to you and pick it up, at the same time praising the dog for 'leaving'. Let the dog then see you drop a few tasty morsels into the bowl and give it back.

This will prove to your dog that you can compel it to 'leave' and also that you sometimes only want the bowl to add a little extra. You can see now why you need to sort out this problem in puppyhood; a fully grown adult who has not learned early that his owner is omnipotent is a very difficult problem.

You *must* win all the time. Take the trouble to think of solutions yourself; you have a superior brain to your dog (at least I hope so), so always be prepared to find sneaky ways to combat your dog's power.

Above: *If you see an obviously aggressive dog approaching do not tense up, as this will tell your dog that you are anxious. Walk on in a relaxed manner.*

Left: *A bone will be a prized possession, but train your dog to allow you to approach and take away its food.*

Aggression with other dogs is another problem, usually found in males rather than females, and although I have seen some aggressive Rottweiler bitches, they are much rarer. It is very hard work to stop adult males from being aggressive if they were not stopped the very first time they showed such tendencies. The best way is to use a check chain.

If you see trouble brewing, for example the approach of a dog not on a lead, *do not* tense up and tighten your lead, as this tells your dog that you are anxious and it will react immediately. Instead, tell your dog to 'leave it' and continue to walk on in a relaxed manner, but be ready. When the other dog is

about 20ft (6m) away and your dog lunges at it, let the weight of your dog going forward meet suddenly with your weight going back (which is the purpose of the loose lead – if the lead is tight you cannot do this). A check chain used in this manner gives the dog a shock and it should be accompanied by a tirade of abuse from you. You *must* be prepared to be hard on your dog for unwarranted aggression.

If your dog knows the words 'down stay', another method is to put your dog in this position upon the approach of a loose dog, and carry in your pocket a spare heavy check chain which you can throw at the other dog if it approaches too closely. This may well enrage the dog's owner, but if he or she cannot keep the dog under control, it is better for you to keep it away than for it to be eaten by your Rottweiler.

You can see now why you need a strong personality to own a

Above: *Leave the check chain loose so that when the dog rushes forward the momentum will serve to create a hard jerk of the chain on the dog's neck.*

Above: *When the dog drops back to the normal walking position offer it plenty of praise and continue walking. Never let aggression pass unchecked.*

Rottweiler, but if you train it correctly from puppyhood these problems will not arise.

As a last resort, you can have your male dog castrated. Some people think this is cruel, but look at it logically. Your average run-of-the-mill Rottweiler male is not likely to be used at stud (nor should it be unless it is an outstanding specimen with an HD-Free Certificate). I know you all think that your dog is the most beautiful Rottweiler in the world, but there is an old saying that goes 'There is only one perfect dog in all the world and every owner has it', and it is very true.

The sex drive is only a nuisance to the average male dog; it is a misguided idea that it will help the dog to mate it once. Since you cannot keep up a supply of females, it is kinder for the dog never to be used. Castration is also sometimes kinder from the point of view that it often stops a great deal of sexually related aggression. You must remember, though, that you should never castrate a dog until it has all its male hormones, ie at about 18 months, or it will stay puppylike. Castration after it has all its male hormones will not make it soppy; the dog's character remains the same, except that it has less desire to fight. You must cut down on the dog's food though, as they have a tendency to put on weight.

Above: *It is vital to keep your dog under control at the vet's. Begin training at puppyhood.*

AGGRESSION TOWARDS PEOPLE

There is another kind of problem which causes a great deal of worry, and this is aggression towards the vet if the dog has to be treated for ailments. This should never be allowed: your vet's hands are his livelihood and many vets do not like to treat our breed because of the few 'wrong 'uns' that try to eat the vet and wreck the surgery. A Rottweiler which is under control and has respect for its owner should be good in all circumstances. However, if you did not teach your dog properly and do not have it under control, how do you deal with the problem of a 'vet hater'? Tranquillizers help, but they need to be given well before the visit; you, the owner, should hold the dog's head and, if necessary, tape the dog's muzzle so that it cannot bite; you should also be ready to give the dog a hard thump if it plays up. Whatever you do, do not ever let your dog bite the vet!

Aggression upon the approach of a stranger is a problem which can be very serious. This has to be stopped or the dog's life may be forfeit. It is not brave or protective – in fact, it is generally the opposite; it is caused by fear or nervous aggression. I do not mean the dog which barks when a stranger knocks at the door, but the dog which hackles up and roars at passers-by in the street when out with its owner. Some people think that this is clever, and that the dog is looking after them. Nothing is further from the truth, as most dogs which do this lack self-confidence and would back off if real trouble came along. Again, this is caused usually by a lack of socialization when the dog was young or, in some cases, it is an inherited tendency. Such dogs must *never* be bred from and, if the dog is truly nervous, it is sometimes kinder to have it put down. Personally, I believe that a nervous Rottweiler is a liability and no pleasure to own. It is also potentially dangerous.

However, if the dog was never socialized, then the behaviour is probably not inherited. It is caused by human error and hard, patient work can improve the dog dramatically. You must take the dog to places where it will see people, traffic, and other everyday sights; sometimes just sitting on a park bench with the dog beside you helps. Training

classes help too.

Dogs which lunge at people must be severely chastised – use the method I described earlier for aggression towards other dogs. You can give the dog a very hard slap for this too: in fact, you cannot be hard enough for this behaviour. Bearing in mind that your dog's life is on the line if it bites people, it sometimes pays to get very tough!

Do not forget, however, that most Rottweilers never need such treatment if raised in the correct manner. I only advocate being tough when the dog really needs it.

There are some owners who become afraid of their own dog. This is a grave problem, since the dog will know this from the scent given out and, if you are really afraid of a dog, it will react to this fear scent and become really dominant. I feel that this is one circumstance where it is sometimes better to part with the dog unless you can get skilled help, both to conquer your fear and to teach the dog properly.

Below: *Aggression may be a sign of lack of socialization. Take your dog out and about to accustom it to people and traffic. In this way it will become a safe and trusted companion for all the family.*

Yet another reason to get your dog under control while it is young!

DEALING WITH STEALING

Stealing is something I am often asked about: stealing food from worktops, dirty washing from bathrooms, clean washing from the line, etc. Stealing is not seen to be a crime by a dog. The desirable object is within reach and there is no dog law which says 'thou shalt not steal'. It is, however, a crime in human eyes, so the dog has to learn this. How do you stop this act? We have a law in our house: the floor is the 'dog shelf' and if any item is left on it then it is our fault if it is taken. This also helps to train the family not to leave a trail of dirty socks around the floor, to pick up toys, etc, so it is a good rule in most homes. However, stealing from high places can be stopped by leaving booby traps.

I once had a dog called Gamegards Fire & Rain (Condor) who, through his film work, had been trained to open cupboard doors. The refrigerator had a door which he could easily open and often when I was outside he would open it and steal the cheese. The problem was not just the theft of the cheese; since no-one was there to tell him to 'shut the door' he left it open. This meant the other house dogs could raid the rest of the contents! My solution was a mouse trap, set with a lump of cheese. I left it at the front of the fridge and went outside, but I hid in a position where I could see the consequences. Sure enough, the clever old lad opened the door and went to take the cheese. What a shock he got when the trap went off and the cheese bit back! It worked well, but I had to leave the trap set for a few more days just in case he tried again. Afterwards, every time he saw a mouse trap he would growl at it.

You can leave booby traps of

meat covered with mustard, or alternatively create a booby trap from a pile of empty beer cans on a bit of cardboard. Put some pebbles in each can and leave the food on a string from the board holding the cans. When the dog takes the food the whole lot comes down on its head –

quite effective. Use your imagination and be inventive. Do not just accept that your dog steals, but think of ways to stop it. Those are some ideas; maybe you can think of better ones.

Washing on the line is a very tempting thing to a young, playful dog, so either put your

Above: *Care should be taken to keep doors closed and 'chewables' out of reach of inquisitive Rottweilers!*

line too high for it to reach, or put it in a place the dog cannot get to. Use plain common sense.

Above: *This is the incorrect way to loop a check chain. It will not loosen when the dog ceases to put pressure upon it so improved behaviour will not be rewarded.*

Below: *The correct way to loop a check chain. It will loosen as soon as the dog ceases to strain against it. Note that the dog must be on your left hand side.*

ADVANCED TRAINING

Now on to more formal training. You need to learn to use a check chain in the correct manner. Use a very strong check chain, and a 4ft (122cm) long lead made of bridle leather and riveted, with a trigger clip. Look at the photographs of the right and wrong way to put on a check chain; it is essential that the chain is on the dog properly, or it

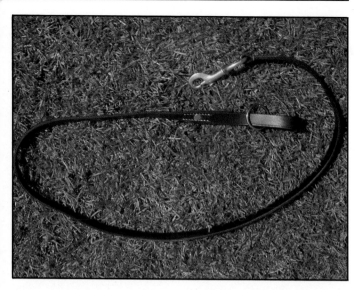

Above: *Choose a strong leash of bridle leather; sewn, riveted and fitted with a trigger clip.*

will not slacken when the pressure is off. The dog, for training purposes, is always on your left hand side because, in competition work, this is always the way it is done.

Your dog should walk at heel with its head about level with your knee or upper thigh, depending on its height. The lead must be loose, as shown in the photograph, and the chain should lie comfortably but very loosely on the neck. When the dog goes to rush ahead or to the side, give a hard, quick, tug on the lead, which will cause the chain suddenly to go tight. It must be almost a snapping motion, as your weight going back meets the dog's weight going forward. Don't just use your wrists or arms – get your shoulders behind the force, too. This action of the loose lead snapping tight will give the dog a shock and you should use the command 'Rex, heel', not forgetting to praise really highly when the dog is back in the correct position.

It is all a matter of good timing – tugging too late when the dog has already taken up the slack in the lead is of no use at all; neither is constantly sawing at the dog's neck with silly little tugs. One good check will show the dog that it is really not worth while to pull on the lead and it will get to love the praise you give it when it does well. (See p.55.)

If you have the opposite problem of the dog hanging back behind you, then go back to a collar and use great encouragement. Keep up a steady stream of chat, such as 'Come on, Rex, what a good little Rex, let's go see what's up here, come Rex', even crouch down and encourage the dog forward. Anything which brings the dog forward in the way of inducement is good. Never, never use force. On a lagging dog it makes the situation worse; you need to build up the dog's confidence, not crush it.

Once the dog has the hang of walking to heel properly, then do a few 'sits'. Walk off, after saying to your dog first, 'Rex, heel', then after a few paces say 'Sit' and press your hand down on the dog's rump, pushing it into the

sitting position. Most dogs, by this time, will know the word 'sit', but you want your dog to sit quickly on the first command when you stop. If you are training for the show ring, when you stop tell your dog to 'stand stay' and spend a few seconds practising with the dog to adopt a good 'stand'; you may use a titbit for this. Some people gently put a foot under the dog's belly to get the idea into the dog's head, but I stress gently. Make the 'stand' command a bit long-drawn-out – 'Staaaand' – and do not use a harsh voice; this word must be encouraging rather than disciplining.

If you are too hard with this exercise the dog will stand like a pile of rice pudding, whereas you want an alert, attentive stand. If you want to enter your dog in shows later, always tell your dog to 'stand' for a titbit from puppyhood instead of the usual method of 'sit'. Once a dog has learned to sit for a reward of this kind it is very difficult to persuade it to stand – the bottom hits the ground all the time and it can be very frustrating for you and the dog.

Above: *When you are training for shows teach your dog to adopt a good 'stand' for the judge.*

When you are out in an open space, for example the park or fields, spend a few minutes doing some 'sit stay' and 'down stay' exercises and recalls before you let your dog run about freely. It takes a very little time and the run afterwards is an excellent reward. One potentially life-saving exercise is to be able to drop your dog into the 'down' position wherever it is.

To teach this exercise, the dog must, of course, know the word 'down' already. Leave him in the 'sit stay' position and walk away about 20 paces, turn and face him, count to five in your head and then call him. When the dog is about a quarter of the way towards you, say, 'Rex, down,' and take a step or two towards him with your arm pointing to the ground. Do it in an urgent manner – pretend there is a bus about to run the dog over if it continues to come. This will give your voice impact, and cause the dog to check its recall. You may

need to repeat the command or even take a few steps closer. When the dog goes down, go up to it and praise very highly. A word of warning: don't do this exercise too much or it will slow down your recall. Just do it occasionally, until in the end when the dog hears 'Rex, down' it will drop like a stone. It is a very worthwhile exercise.

Above: *When on a walk allow your dog to enjoy its exercise and do not give commands unnecessarily.*

SUMMING UP

One fault I notice with many would-be trainers is that of nagging when the dog is free and out at exercise. Do try not to do this, or your dog will quickly become bored and soon will ignore your commands because it incessantly hears 'Rex come', 'Rex leave', etc. Call your dog when necessary, of course, but do not keep calling. Let your dog have some peace to sniff and enjoy its walk, but keep an eye open all the time for hazards such as an obviously aggressive dog, farm animals, or even perhaps the sight in the distance of a person wearing a floppy macintosh which, to a young inexperienced dog, might look

threatening enough for it to want to bark. Get to know your dog's mind, be one step ahead.

You must be confident that you can control your dog at all times, and of course if you did your homework you will be.

So let us re-cap: *Do* be positive, confident, firm, fun and determined; *Do not* nag, dither, or lose your temper.

Learn how to use your voice clearly so that it conveys the correct message to your dog. Dull monotones are out. Use feeling in the voice – aim for venom and honey!

Enjoy your training, enjoy your dog, and *always win*. If you need help from a more experienced trainer, ask for it, and never be afraid to make haste slowly or go back a step. Never encourage your dog to be aggressive.

Chapter Four

HEALTH PROBLEMS

Hip displaysia
Osteochondrosis
Cruciate ligament
Contagious diseases
Eye problems
Skin problems
Enzyme deficiency
Bloat
Inoculations

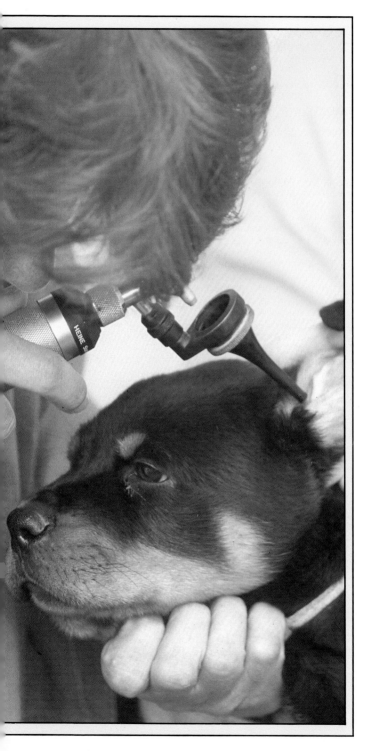

HIP DYSPLASIA

Hip dysplasia (HD) is one of the biggest problems to beset Rottweilers. It is a malformation of the ball and socket joint of the hip – sometimes the cup or, to give it its correct name, the acetabulum, is too shallow, or the ball or femoral head may be misshapen, and this will cause a great deal of pain and arthritis in later life. This distressing condition is thought to be 40 per cent inherited, hence my constant urging for all breeding animals to be hip scored through the hip scheme for the relevant country; only by X-ray can you tell what the hips are like, as you cannot see by the dog's movement unless it is a very bad case. For control schemes, X-rays are done under general anaesthetic at one year. Under the hip scoring scheme, the minimum score for each hip

is 0 and the maximum 53; the lower the score, the less the degree of hip dysplasia. The range is thus 0–106 for both hips. A total score of 0–4 (with not more than 3 for one hip) is acceptable, while a score of 5–8 (with not more than 6 for one hip) would indicate that the dog can breed, but its mate must have a lower score. The breed norm score at this time is 14 in the UK.

In the United States a control scheme is run by the Orthopedic Foundation for Animals (O.F.A.). This organization checks a dog's X-rays and pronounces it afflicted or not afflicted. If HD-free, the animal is given an O.F.A. registration number.

HD is a condition that can be controlled by selective breeding

Below: *An X-ray of the hips of a dog with dysplasia. Note misshapen joint. Selective breeding could help stop this.*

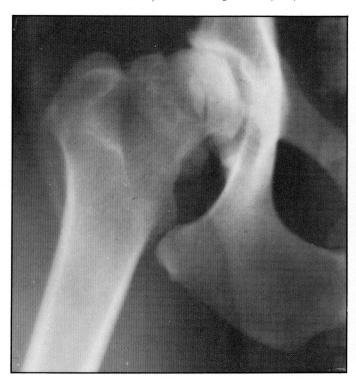

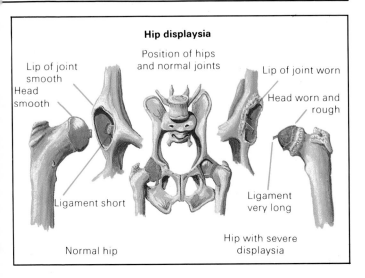

Hip displaysia

Position of hips and normal joints

Lip of joint smooth

Head smooth

Lip of joint worn

Head worn and rough

Ligament short

Ligament very long

Normal hip

Hip with severe displaysia

and careful rearing, so please do not breed from un-X-rayed Rottweilers and do not buy a pup unless you can see the official hip scores.

If you are unlucky enough to own an affected dog, there are surgical procedures which can help. The femoral head can be removed or, in some cases, the pectinious muscle can be cut, which causes the joint to pull apart, alleviating some pain. However this method is not 100 per cent effective, and there are now other operations that are more successful.

OSTEOCHONDROSIS

This is another orthopaedic condition, the cause of which is at present not known. It can affect the shoulder, elbow, hock or stifle joints during the growing period. Bits of cartilage grow and sometimes flake off into the joint, causing a lot of pain and usually necessitating surgery to remove the cartilage pieces.

Any lameness during puppyhood should be investigated by your vet, and rest is essential to minimize the damage. I have had five cases during the last few years, all from different litters, and in four cases

Above: *Shown from below, with legs pushed back: a normal hip compared with one with HD.*

the owners of the puppies had cars with high backs, so there may be a case for making a connection between jumping in and out of high places and osteochondrosis.

CRUCIATE LIGAMENT

This is the cross ligament which runs through the stifle joint (equivalent to our knee), and it can snap or stretch. The dog will carry its leg in a very peculiar manner with the toe pointing to the ground. This, too, needs surgery and fairly quickly, before secondary changes make the damage worse. The dog needs very careful nursing afterwards, being taken on a lead to relieve itself and allowed no other exercise until the leg is strong again. There do seem to be some bloodlines in which this condition occurs more often; my own theory is that it seems to happen more often with the short coupled, very tightly-knit dogs with little hind angulation.

I have only had two cases in 25 years: one in my very first

Rottweiler who, at the age of nine, was hit sideways on by another Rottweiler running really fast. There was a crash of bodies and my dog was lamed; he was operated on and made a full recovery. The second case was a female, aged eight, who jumped a ditch and landed badly. She too had snapped a cruciate, but, after surgery, made a full recovery.

CONTAGIOUS DISEASES

Leptospirosis, hardpad, distemper, hepatitis and parvo virus are the big five killer diseases, with parvo virus the most virulent to our breed. It is essential that all dogs be inoculated at 12 weeks, and boosted annually.

Sickness, diarrhoea (with a never-to-be-forgotten smell) and listlessness should be treated immediately by your vet if the dog has any chance of survival: this is parvo virus. You cannot imagine how quickly a healthy puppy could be transformed into a dehydrated dying skeleton in two or three days: please never underestimate the value of inoculations for this dreaded disease.

EYE PROBLEMS

Entropion, or inturning eyelids, is usually found in dogs with deepset eyes and with too much loose skin on the head. It causes pain and may even ulcerate the eye, so consult your vet and have the eye operated on. Do not ignore it, as it will not go away on its own. It is an inherited condition, so do not breed from affected animals.

Conjunctivitis is an infection which causes yellow runny eyes. Your vet will give you an antibiotic ointment which will soon clear it up.

EAR MITES

Brownish secretions in the ear usually mean ear mites. They itch badly, especially when the dog is hot. Do not put just any ear powder in the ear, but get the correct medication from your vet and use it diligently. Check your cats, too, as they get ear mites and will re-infect your dog.

SKIN PROBLEMS

Eczema can be flea-induced and the dog will bite at the base of the tail, causing great raw weeping patches. First get rid of the fleas using a collar or pet spray on the dog and treating the house, where the flea eggs and larvae live, with an IGR (insect growth regulator) product available from pet shops. Bath your dog in a good anti-flea shampoo, then paint the eczema with gentian violet – it

Below: *Entropion (inturning) eyelids can cause great distress and may need surgery.*

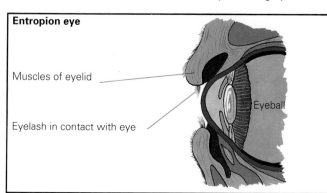

Entropion eye

Muscles of eyelid

Eyeball

Eyelash in contact with eye

tastes horrible, stings a lot, stops the itch and dries up the wet patches. Sometimes play bites on the face will flare up into eczema – use gentian violet again, or get a proprietory cream from the vet.

Mange is another case for the vet. A skin scraping may be taken to ascertain whether it is sarcoptic or follicular mange; both need baths and very careful treatment. It is fairly rare in Rottweilers. An old cure is sump (crankcase) oil and sulphur: empty the used oil from the car sump (crankcase), mix it with yellow flowers of sulphur powder and cover all affected areas well beyond the actual baldness. Keep the dog in a place where it cannot rub on furniture or ruin your decor, as it is very messy. Do it daily for three weeks and it will work like magic. You must always consult your vet as well to be on the safe side.

Below: *Allergic reactions can cause itchy paws. Dogs must be stopped from gnawing them.*

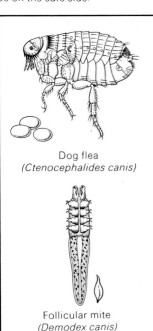

Dog flea
(Ctenocephalides canis)

Follicular mite
(Demodex canis)

Above: *Two types of external parasites with their eggs. Too small to be seen, their effects on a dog can be obvious.*

FEET

Some Rottweilers get itchy feet, when they bite and chew until the pads are raw. I think that my own dogs are allergic to some carpet-cleaning powders. I have cured this with a product called Bitter Apple, which stops them chewing immediately.

ENZYME DEFICIENCY

Some Rottweilers do not produce enough enzymes from the pancreas, in which case they fail to body up, have loose motions and are not able to digest fat. If your dog has these symptoms take a sample of faeces to your vet for analysis; the condition can be controlled by adding a pancreatic extract to the diet.

CANCER

This is a condition which sometimes strikes the breed. When it is diagnosed my solution is to give the dog a good end, before it becomes racked with pain. Treatment, in my experience, is seldom successful and I cannot bear to have a dog die slowly and painfully. It is kinder to let the dog quietly go to sleep in your arms with a little help from the vet's needle.

BLOAT

Overfeeding, especially with dry foods, can cause the stomach to swell, twist and kill the dog. A good tip, if your dog is blown up, is to give a walnut-sized knob of common washing soda; if the dog is sick within a few minutes then it is not bloat, as they cannot be sick with true bloat. If the dog is not sick, then get it to the vet *fast*. The remedy is surgical, and seconds are vital if the life of the dog is to be saved.

Below: *Don't risk your pet's life by neglecting vital inoculations. Rottweilers are prone to parvo virus, which can be fatal.*

INOCULATIONS

Rottweilers are very prone to parvo virus (see p.68), so please ensure that your inoculations are kept up to date. The earliest date at which my vet will inoculate is nine weeks, with a second course two weeks later. This allows you to get your pup socialisation done as soon as possible, but be careful to check just how long after the last shots you must wait for the serum to take full effect.

Nowadays the vaccines are of a very high standard and you will need the full course for distemper, hard pad, leptospirosis, hepatitus and parvo virus. Some vets will give your dog protection against

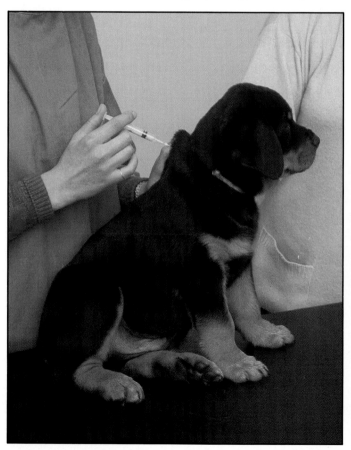

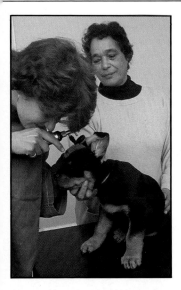

Above: *Your dog should become used to being handled by a vet. Never, ever allow aggression.*

kennel cough as well. Kennel cough has many strains and it is difficult to find one answer to all of them. It is not a dangerous virus in healthy dogs, but you should watch for secondary infections in young or older dogs and seek treatment; it will usually last three weeks.

Your vet will normally send you a reminder card when annual boosters are due, but to be on the safe side you should enter the dates in your diary. Boosters are well worth the expense and could save your pet's life.

In the USA, rabies shots are required in every state. Pups can be given these shots at three months and this will provide protection for one year. After the second shot at fifteen months, boosters will be required every three years. You will be given a record card of all your shots by the vet and this should be kept in a safe place and taken along to the vet's at the time of annual boosters so that it is kept up to date. Should you need to put your dog into a boarding kennel you will need to produce this card, as no reputable kennel will accept a dog without proof of inoculation.

GENERAL

Basically, the Rottweiler is a fairly healthy breed, but remember that prevention is better than cure: check your dog for parasites, use common sense when out at exercise. Don't fatten puppies, keep them lean, feed them well, but don't over-feed. Keep your eyes open and know your dog well, for a slight change in behaviour could mean that the dog is in pain. Make friends with your vet and be sure your dog does too. You may not need to see the vet often, but when you do be fair to him, telling him all the symptoms clearly, and never call for night visits unless it is a real emergency.

Checklist for health

(a) Feed well, but don't indulge the dog until it gets fat
(b) Don't give 'sweeties'. If you use a titbit for training, hard-bake some little bits of liver, the most popular treat of all
(c) Exercise mind as well as body
(d) Keep all inoculations up to date
(e) Never ignore symptoms of illness
(f) If you get a problem, consult your breeder or vet

(g) Keep an eye open at all times for parasites; fleas, lice and worms. Deal with them immediately
(h) Watch that claws don't grow too long

Maintaining any dog is a matter of common sense and a little know how: I hope that you already possess the common sense and that I have given you, in this small table, at least a little know how.

Chapter Five

BREEDING THE ROTTWEILER

Choosing a bitch
Choosing a stud
Mating
Whelping
The first weeks

CHOOSING A BITCH

If everyone bred a litter 'because it is good for the bitch', we should all be knee-deep in puppies.

There are several reasons to breed a bitch: if she is a really good specimen of the breed, if she has a perfect temperament and if she X-rayed well under the official scheme. However, you should only breed your bitch if you have the time to give to the pups, the money to raise them well and the space to keep them. They may not all be sold until three or four months old and, at that age, they eat a lot and need inoculations, attention and socialization.

You must be in a position to take back any of your pups if they need to be re-homed. You are responsible for bringing that dog into the world so you must be prepared to help it if necessary. You should also be able to advise your puppy buyers on all aspects of rearing and training, and be at the end of the telephone when they need help.

Many people breed a litter for the money but, if the job is done properly, there is not much profit in it. Most caring breeders like

Below: *Sire with puppies aged seven weeks. Now is the time when socialization should begin in earnest; helped by dad's fine example!*

myself have to work to pay for the cost of keeping their dogs – in my case it is my film and television work with dogs which pays for their keep, one other breeder is a night nurse and yet another works in a garage as a petrol pump attendant, so you can see it is not the way to a fortune!

Whelping kennels have to be lined with good insulating material so that the kennel is draught-proof, and there must be a heater over the whelping box. In very cold weather you may need an extra heater, as newly born pups soon get chilled and will die very quickly; this is all expensive.

However, let us start at the beginning – you have a good quality well-bred bitch, she has a good character, and has X-rayed well. You realize the responsibilities of breeding and are prepared to keep the pups over a period of time if need be, and to vet prospective owners carefully. You have learned something of breed requirements so that you can help and advise the new owners.

CHOOSING A STUD

How to find the best male dog for your bitch? If you already own a male there is the temptation to use him or the dog of a friend nearby. My advice is don't: it is rare that your own dog or a neighbour's dog will suit your bitch in terms of conformation, blood line or anything else. Attend a few shows months before you intend to mate your bitch, get your eye in, and learn correct type. Visit well-known reputable breeders, too, look at their stud dogs and take your pedigree to compare. Know your own bitch's failings and virtues and choose wisely: it is very important that the stud dog has a good hip score, too, and ask about his parents' and grandparents' scores, as the better the background the better

Above: *A view of whelping kennels. Note how clean and tidy they are kept. Each bitch has her own kennel for privacy. An interior is shown on p.78.*

the chance of good hips. Make sure that the stud dog has a good character. If you cannot handle the dog suspect the worst, as many people try to mask a nasty temperament by making excuses. Beware of this, as a dog with good character should be able to be touched.

It is a wise idea to have a vaginal swab done by your vet a few weeks before your bitch is due in season. It is amazing how many bitches have a B.H.S. (beta haemolytic streptococcus) infection which will cause weak, fading puppies, but it is easily removed with a course of an appropriate antibiotic. I have my studs swabbed regularly too, because a visiting bitch could easily infect them. You should also check your bitch for hookworm.

Be prepared to travel a fair distance if need be. Do not select the nearest stud simply because it happens to be conveniently close to home.

MATING

So now you have chosen the dog and booked the provisional mating with the owner. Stud fees are usually the price of a pet puppy, but may vary from country to country and according to the dog's merit. Be sure you know the stud fee well in advance as it is normally paid at the time of the service, although some people will accept a puppy in lieu of a stud fee.

I like to try the bitch about the tenth day from the first signs of season – this may be too early for some bitches, but some are ovulating at this time and the correct day varies from bitch to bitch. If she will not 'stand' for the dog, then try her on the twelfth day and again on the fourteenth day. When a bitch is ready she will allow the dog to lick her vulva with evident enjoyment and will curl her tail to one side. Some maiden bitches will love the preliminaries but snap if the dog tries to mount them. This is where the stud owner (usually an experienced breeder) must define whether your bitch is just being 'touch me not', is not ready, or is past the correct time. I find that my own male dogs tell me if a bitch is ready or not by their attitude and behaviour. Sometimes the bitch

Top: *The dogs will become acquainted by engaging in a playful 'courting' session.*

Middle: *The bitch will signal her willingness to mate by presenting her rear end to the dog.*

Bottom: *The dog will mount the bitch and effect a 'tie', with his penis swelling inside her.*

Right: *The dog will
then turn his back to
the bitch. A maiden
bitch may panic, so
hold her firmly by the
collar.*

Below: *The dogs will
remain in the mating
position for 5 – 45
minutes. Do not let
them wander about
during this period.*

is willing to mate if the owner is
not looking. It sounds silly, but
there are bitches who are so
'humanized' and devoid of
instinct that they think it is
naughty to allow such liberties.

It is important that the dog
'courts' the bitch. A little foreplay
will often stimulate the bitch but
too much will tire out the dog, so
let them just get to know each
other. When the dog actually
mounts the bitch, hold her collar
so that she does not turn and
snap at the crucial moment. A
collar is important when mating a
bitch, as you need something
more solid than a check chain to
hang on to. Once the dog has
entered the bitch he will swell up
inside her and effect a 'tie', so
that they cannot part until the
dog's penis has gone down
again. Some maiden bitches
panic, so it is important to hold
her firmly and not let her thrash
about, which could damage her

and the dog. The male will turn
round until they are back to back
and there they remain for 5-45
minutes, until the 'tie' is over. It is
always advisable to hold them
both at this point as they will
often attempt to wander about in
this position and make
themselves very uncomfortable.

Once the pair have separated a
fair amount of fluid will come out
of the bitch. Do not worry, as this
is just flushing fluid – the actual
semen is well on its way to do the
job. There is absolutely no need
to hold up the bitch's back legs
like a wheelbarrow, as I have
seen some people do or, even
worse, spit on the hand and slap
it on the bitch's vulva to 'seal it'.

It is advisable to have two
matings about 48 hours apart.
This will ensure the fertilization
of the eggs, since the sperm lives
for at least 24 hours within the
bitch and so this covers you for
at least a four day period.

WHELPING

Until the bitch starts to show 'in whelp' at about five to six weeks treat her as normal, giving perhaps a little extra calcium and vitamin supplement. Later on she will have to have smaller meals and be fed twice or even thrice daily. Be sure that she has good nourishing food, but do not let her pack on the fat. Walks will be steadier as she will not feel like leaping about, so let her go at her own pace and keep her fit.

Your whelping area should be ready, with the whelping box in place, and she should be encouraged to use the area and box to sleep in. Some bitches dig holes when pregnant. This is the nest-building instinct at work, so do not scold her if she digs up your flowers – the force telling her to do it is very strong and she will become upset. Just plant a few more flowers and see things in perspective.

As the sixty-third day approaches you may see a white mucus discharge from the vulva. This is normal so do not worry. The temperature of the bitch will drop from 101°F (38°C) to 99°F (37°C) or 98°F (36.5°C) the day before whelping, and she will tear up her bedding. Some bitches refuse to eat the day before whelping but Rottweilers are often so greedy that they eat as normal. Have a bottle of

disinfectant for sterilizing, clean towels, scissors and lots of clean newspapers in readiness for the birth, plus a cardboard box and a hot water bottle just in case you need it for the puppies. It is a good idea to tell your vet when the bitch is due so that he can be on standby if needed. I usually have a pack of puppy milk and a baby's bottle and teat just in case her milk is late, or she needs help with feeding a large litter.

As zero hour approaches the bitch will be restless, panting, tearing up her bed, circling round and looking at her rear end apprehensively, interspersed with periods of calm. It is essential that you do not get nervous; sit quietly with her,

speaking in a calm, confident voice, watch and wait. Do not invite in the neighbours to spectate, and do not rush about and panic – this is a normal, natural event and your little expectant mum will do a good job so long as you do not fuss too much. The first sign of an approaching puppy will be some strong pushes from the bitch, followed soon after by either a bubble of foetal membrane or the pup itself. Most bitches expel their pups easily, but some will be born hindfirst and you may well have to grip the back legs of the pup with a clean towel and wait until the next push before *gently* helping the pup into the world. Most births in this breed are relatively easy but a useful tip is not to let the bitch go more than three hours between pups if she is straining and pushing. This usually means problems, so call your vet.

When the pup is born the bitch will bite the cord, eat the placenta and clean up the pup. Sometimes maiden bitches will not do this, so cut the cord with sterile scissors and rub the pup with a clean towel, giving it a little shake nose down to remove any mucus from the nasal passages, then present the pup to the mother again. If she is not interested, pop the puppy into a cardboard box with a clean towel over a hot water bottle and put it in a warm place – she will accept it later on when she has finished whelping. You may have to give her a firm command to lie down and let them all suckel, but she will soon settle as long as you do not interfere too much. Newly born pups need heat and food, and cannot urinate or defecate without stimulation, hence the mother's constant licking.

Left: *A pregnant bitch becoming accustomed to the whelping box. Note the 'pig rail' to prevent the mother from accidentally squashing the pups.*

THE FIRST WEEKS

Your bitch will need light, milky feeds with scrambled eggs and a little cereal for the first few days. Do not worry if she has loose black motions, as this is the normal result of eating the afterbirths (placentas), which are very rich in iron. Make sure she always has water to drink – lactating bitches need a lot of fluids and, as the pups grow, increase her food intake and provide plenty of milk as well. Some of my bitches almost treble their normal food intake spread over two or three meals when they are feeding pups. It is sensible to let the vet check her over after the birth to ensure that there are no retained puppies or

Below: *Mothers stand to give milk during the latter stage of the lactation period.*

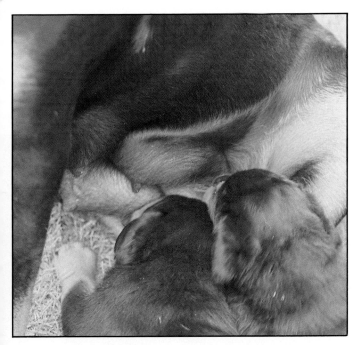

Above: *Their mother's milk is best for puppies, providing them with vital nutrients.*

placentas which would quickly cause her temperature to rise and can create great problems. Ask the vet to check the pups for malformations, such as cleft palates, or other problems.

At three to four days the tails need to be docked and the dew claws removed. The procedure of tail docking is no longer allowed to be carried out by lay people in the UK. Vets are still permitted to perform this, however many are anti-docking. If you want your litter docked, you are advised to find a vet willing to do this before even mating your bitch. The dew claws I remove with sharp sterilized scissors puffing on an antibotic powder to prevent infection and clot the blood quickly. If in doubt ask your vet or an experienced breeder to do it as it is not really a novice's job. It is best to take your bitch out when this is done as it will upset her.

You may find that one or two pups are pushed to a far corner of the box by their mother and they usually appear to be cold and feeble. I wish I could tell you that

they will be all right but usually, if the mother rejects them, there is a reason – they do not smell right and she knows better than us. I never try to revive feeble puppies. Do you really want to keep pups which are likely to be sickly, weedy dogs? In a very large litter you have a choice either to cull some of them or bottle feed at two-hourly intervals, since some will die anyway from lack of food.

Bottle feeding is hard work and, as the pups get maternal immunity from the colostrum, or first milk, they all need to have it. It is best to feed half the litter on bottle milk for one feed and allow the other half to feed from the mother, then alternate at the next feed, making sure that every pup gets that essential mother's milk. The bitch still needs peace and quiet at this stage, so do not bring friends and relatives in to view the pups until they are older, or she will become agitated.

At three weeks of age you can start to wean a large litter (four weeks if it is a small one). Begin with a little milky cereal – finely ground oats with an egg yolk or two is good – or scrambled egg.

The pups will make a mess at first but within two or three days they will get used to eating. Food for weaning must be like a purée with no lumps. At six weeks your puppies will eat minced cooked meat and cereal or flaked fish with cereal, and you can use cooked eggs, too. Four feeds a

Left: *A good mother checking up on two of her puppies. In their game they are showing typical dominant/submissive postures.*

Above: *For the first eight weeks the mother dominates the puppy's life; after this the puppy can be found a new home.*

day are required and do not forget to give puppy milk or fresh goats' milk as cows' milk will often scour them for some reason. Always remember the golden rule – do not let them get fat. People ask what they should weigh at various ages and I have heard all sorts of answers to this question. My own view is that if they look good, well-covered but not fat, if they eat well and have lots of energy, and if they are well-boned and healthy, they are the right weight. If you develop a good eye for livestock you should see for yourself what physical condition they are in.

Worm them at four, six and eight weeks and pick up the puppies' droppings several times a day, especially when they have just been wormed. If you do not do this the pups will roll over in droppings when they play and

get very smelly and messy, and may also become re-infected.

The pups will be ready to go to their new homes at eight weeks. When prospective owners come, check that they have a responsible person at home all day and that they have a large outside area which is well fenced. Do not forget to tell them all the problems which can arise in this breed and how to deal with them, and – very important – check that the prospective owners have firm, sensible temperaments and want the dog for the right reasons.

Give a diet sheet (see p.88), and perhaps even a few days' supply of the food to which the puppy is used. If your registrations are back from the Kennel Club be sure to give them, as well as the pedigree; if not, send them on later.

Chapter Six

FEEDING AND CARE

Obesity
Grooming
Worming
Line and inbreeding

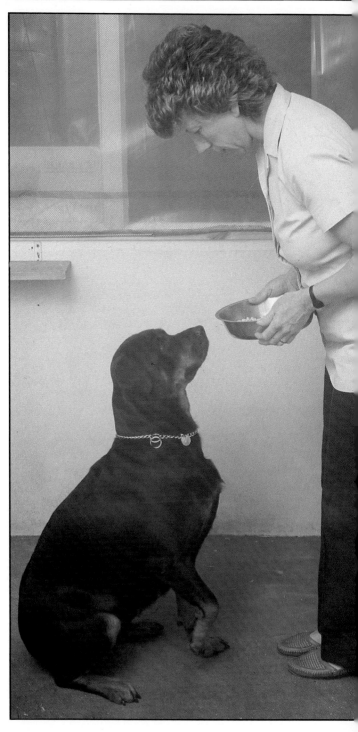

OBESITY

Within any breed there are dogs that need more or less food than others, and the Rottweiler is no exception. For example, a dog which lies around the house all day will need fewer calories than a breeding animal or a dog which works or takes a great deal of exercise. My daughter has a large stable of horses and her Rottweiler does over 20 miles (32km) a day accompanying rides: he is quite a small male (about 25in (63cm) to the shoulder) but he eats far more than my house male 'Max', who is very much bigger.

It is important, therefore, to calculate roughly how many calories your own dog needs. A good rule is the less exercise, the less food. Most pet Rottweilers are much too fat: their owners are cutting their lifespan with overfeeding or, as my father used to say, 'letting them dig their own grave with their teeth!' It is a sad fact that people seldom realize or accept that their dog is fat; the wisest way is to consult your vet if you want an honest opinion.

Most vets hate obesity in animals, much preferring to see a dog really lean and this is only common sense, because fatness brings a whole set of problems. Try to look at your dog dispassionately. Can you feel its ribs easily? If not, it is probably too fat. You can buy obesity diets from your vet or you can cut the dog's carbohydrate ration in half and gradually step up the amount of exercise he gets. Within three months you will have a much fitter dog. I give my dogs a fasting day every now and then if I see extra pounds creeping on – it helps a lot.

One often sees advertisements for puppies where the father is

stated to be 15 stones (210 lb, 95kg) and the mother 13 stones (182lb, 83kg). It is absolutely crazy to allow Rottweilers to reach that kind of weight. Remember always that this is a working breed, not a contender for the best beef cattle at a stock show!

So what should we feed our dogs? Scientists and nutritionists tell us that the average dog can manage very well on about 18 – 20 per cent of protein daily, so various companies manufacture well-formulated dried foods which you can mix with water to give a good diet. There are dozens of these all-in-one diets and it is important to select one which suits your dog. The one I use is 19.5 per cent protein: it is fortified with vitamins and minerals and I find my dogs do really well on it, so I never give them a change of diet since any changes are liable to cause loose motions.

It is only a human idea to give dogs variety in diet: in the wild there would not be much diversity – just some meat, bones and offal every day. Nowadays, with protein so expensive, it is sensible to cut down on meat and give cheaper forms of protein. As long as the dogs do well on it, there should be no problem. For example, I would feed an adult male Rottweiler taking moderate exercise about three-quarters all-in-one diet to one-quarter protein (this can be fish, hard boiled eggs or pet mince).

In the winter dogs which live outside need more food (and deeper, warmer bedding) to keep out the cold. I do not mind if mine are a few pounds overweight in winter, but come the springtime I adjust their diet until they look good again.

A growing puppy at eight weeks I feed all-in-one, mixed with a good quality puppy milk or goats' milk for the first feed. The next feed is two-thirds all-in-one, well soaked in gravy, to one-third

Left: *Rottweilers tend to be greedy dogs, so must learn to wait patiently for dinner.*

protein (fish, eggs or meat). Then I repeat these two feeds for the third and fourth meals. Check the label on the packing – if you are feeding a very high protein feed you may not need to add anything at all since too much protein is bad for a dog.

A rough guide as to quantities: as I suggested earlier, feed about the size of the dog's head per meal. This works well until you get a dog with either a really overdone huge head or a tiny pin-head. In either case you use common sense again, giving the huge headed one a little less and the pin-head a little more. I never weigh anything – food, dogs or pups – since I like to gauge by eye. If the dog looks good, is fit not fat, and has lots of energy, then you are feeding correctly. There is no time in my day to be forever weighing things; if I have some spare time then I prefer to spend it either training or playing with a pup.

At three months the puppies go on to three feeds a day (obviously slightly larger quantities) and at six months two feeds of even larger quantities per meal. At one year the ration is one meal daily, although this may vary according to the dog's needs. Pregnant bitches, as they advance into their sixth or seventh week, need to eat twice or sometimes three times daily as the pups take up a lot of room and the stomach cannot expand as much. Don't forget that Rottweilers in general are very greedy and will often insist that they just have to have that sandwich you are eating or they will fade away and die from starvation! Don't give in to such transparent lies; don't feed between meals and don't buy 'choc drops' or other junk foods for your dog. If you want to give the dog a real treat, buy marrow bones for it or go out for an extra walk – better for you and far better for the dog.

Another food popular with dog owners is tripe (beef stomach).

This is fine, as long as you remember that tripe is lacking in the essential minerals – calcium and iron; can contain a lot of fat and is not suitable as a complete diet. If you use it, you must give carbohydrate and add the iron and calcium it lacks, so provide a chunk of cooked liver daily and a tablespoonful of bone meal, together with some wholemeal biscuit or all-in-one meal. I never use tripe to feed pups as I like to fill them with good, nourishing, growing food, and tripe is not the

best for this purpose.

Raw meat, especially lamb or pork, is very dangerous as it can give your dog tapeworm, porcine herpes virus or salmonella poisoning. Always bring meat to the boil to sterilize it and never ever feed bones which are liable to splinter, causing perforation of the dog's gut. Be careful to boil the meat thoroughly. Part boiling wil do no good. A pressure cooker is useful to boil down fish pieces and you can even feed the bones as they will be almost

Above: *Feed your puppies from individual dishes to ensure fair distribution. A table will discourage the pups from turning out their feet.*

disintegrated by pressure cooking. This is a good source of calcium. Breast of lamb is good cooked in this way as the bones go soft; you can skim off the fat and feed all the rest.

Canned meats mixed with biscuit are very popular, but I

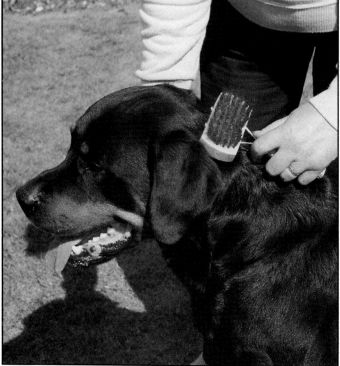

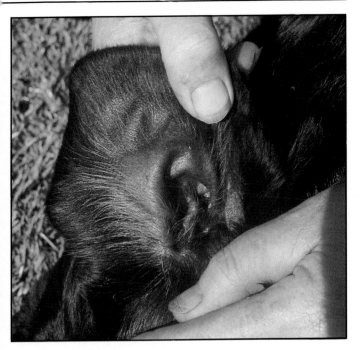

Above: *Check inside the ears every week for embedded grass seeds or signs of ear mites. Both can cause trouble.*

Top left: *Give your dog a good brush every week to keep the coat shining. During the moult, groom every day.*

Bottom left: *A double-sided brush, with wire on one side and rubber bristles on the other, is an ideal grooming tool.*

find this diet very expensive and, in my own dogs, it causes a great deal of flatulence, so I have to give charcoal granules to combat this.

Adult Rottweilers can have table scraps added to their meal, and if you have any stale wholemeal bread pop it into the oven until it bakes hard – they love it! If you want to keep a glossy coat on your dog, give a small piece of polyunsaturated margarine daily (about the size of the top of your little finger).

Never feed sugary substances and don't allow your dog to develop a sweet tooth. Mine will not eat sweets as they have never formed a liking for them, and that's the way I like to keep things.

Some Rottweilers have a taste for fruit and this means they must need extra Vitamin C, so give them a little fruit (for example orange) daily. I have one dog who would eat several oranges if I let him, and he adores melon, too.

GROOMING

I have found that if you feed well you need only give the dog a good brush weekly to keep the coat shining, although during the moult it is as well to have a daily grooming session to remove the dead hair. A rubber cat brush works well and, during the moult, I gently use a metal claw brush to take out dead undercoat, finishing off with a damp chamois leather to add a glossy finish to the coat.

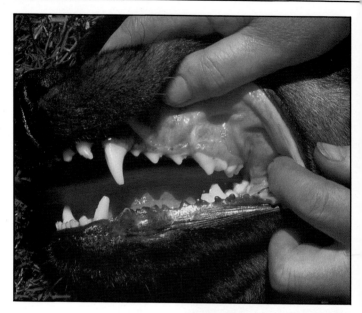

Ears need to be examined weekly for signs of ear mites and a drop or two of a good anti-mite lotion (from your vet) inserted if there are any brown secretions.

If your dog's teeth are full of tartar you can use a toothbrush and doggy toothpaste. I find most dogs hate this procedure, but will put up with it. However, I use the edge of a milled coin to scrape it off very gently, taking care not to make the gums bleed. Marrow bones will prevent much of this problem because the very act of eating them removes such deposits on the teeth. In extreme cases your vet will clean the teeth, possibly with the aid of an anaesthetic for difficult dogs.

If your dog has good feet you will never need to cut the claws; sadly, not all do and some dogs need to have the claws trimmed from time to time. Use the guillotine-type clippers, which do not pinch the quick of the nail. The claws on Rottweilers are black and you cannot see the quick, so a little and often is better than cutting a lot and making the quick bleed. If it does don't worry, as the bleeding will soon stop. You can puff a little

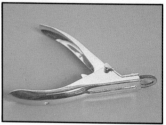

Top: *Your dog's teeth should be checked regularly for tartar. A serious build-up could mean a visit to the vet.*

Above: *Claws are best cut using a pair of guillotine clippers. They cause a dog the minimum of aggravation.*

sulphonilamide powder on the claw to help the blood clot and prevent infection, or you can use friar's balsam. Some people file their dog's claws with a rasp, but I find that clipping is easier for the dog. Exercise on hard surfaces also helps to keep claws short, so try road walking. This also tones up the muscles, especially if it is done at a brisk pace and not an amble.

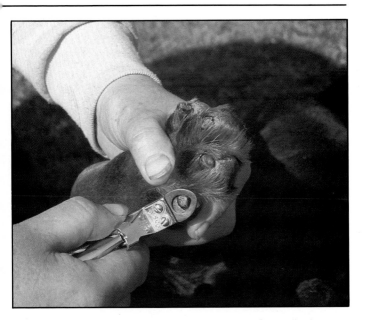

Above: *Care must be taken not to cut the claw's quick. To avoid making it bleed, trim only a little off at a time.*

Below: *If your Rottweiler has been bred with good tight feet, then cutting claws should never really be necessary.*

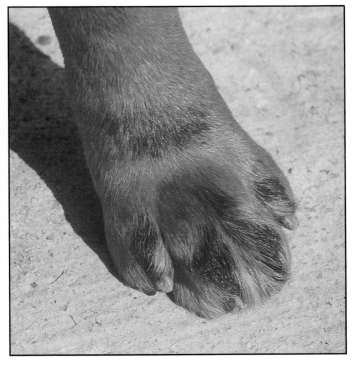

EXERCISING

It is very common in Europe for owners to ride bicycles, the dog following behind, but there is a tendency to do too much too soon. *Never* take a Rottweiler out with a bicycle until it is over one year old and already in good condition: do just a little daily until it is really fit, and make sure that you keep the dog away from danger, such as traffic.

There is one handler/owner in Germany who is well over 60 years old, and he jogs with his dog for two hours daily. They are a joy to see in the show ring, both supremely fit and bursting with health and vitality; they can easily outrun most other Rottweilers and handlers and the rapport between them is wonderful.

But remember, no hard exercise until that first year is over, and get your dog fit gradually. There is a section of the population which leaves the dog lounging around the house all week, then goes for five-hour runs at weekends. They are surprised when their dog cannot walk properly on Monday morning.

This breed is not demanding of exercise, but they do enjoy it, so try to make time each day for you and your dog to have a walk or two.

WORMING

Worming needs to be done on a regular basis and during puppyhood it should take place several times, since roundworms

Below: *Puppies playing in the garden at will can rest when they become tired.*

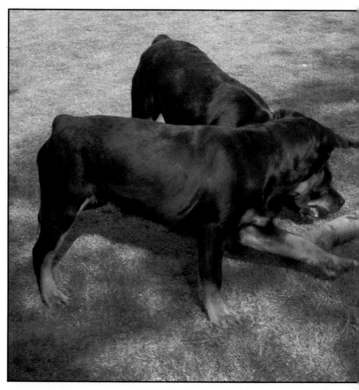

will keep a puppy in poor shape at best and kill it at worst. Adults should be wormed every three months, since they can pick up roundworm larvae from sniffing the excrement of other dogs. It is cheap and easy to worm a dog and it is always best to buy a medicine from your vet.

The public outcry of late about roundworm larvae causing blindness in children does have basis in fact, but do not panic. If your dog is wormed regularly the chance of your child suffering is about the same as the chance of it being sat on by an elephant! Naturally, do not let your dog lick the child's mouth or hands, and make the child wash the hands if they have been licked.

Tapeworm, which is transmitted by fleas and raw meat, affects some dogs. It looks like grains of rice adhering to the dog's anal area and when you see them go straight to the vet

and dose for tapeworm. There is no disgrace in having them, but there is disgrace in leaving them there!

Heartworm, transmitted by mosquitoes, is a problem in some countries. This needs a daily pill to keep it away – consult your vet as to the vermicides required for your area.

Check a bitch for hookworms before breeding from her. These can be deadly if passed on to pups and are very debilitating in older dogs; veterinary care is essential to combat them.

Never ignore worms: they cause a lot of problems, so it is always best to worm regularly as prevention is better than cure for both the dog and you.

Below: *An egg and the first larval stage of the roundworm. Worm regularly to ensure that your dog is free of them.*

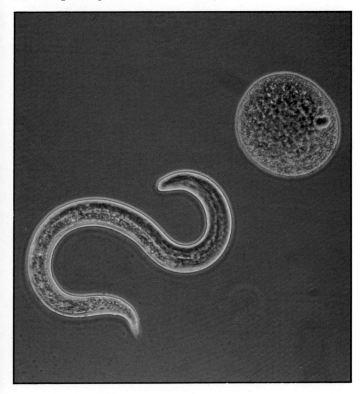

LINE AND INBREEDING

There is a great difference between line breeding and inbreeding. Line breeding is the selection of the best dogs in the line and breeding back to them, eg, granddaughter to grandson, or perhaps great-grandson to granddaughter, thus doubling up on the best lines. Below is the pedigree of a line bred bitch of mine which has produced a very good litter.

It is, however, very important when undertaking this to know what you are doing, and what the animals were like – inside and out. Doubling up on good temperament and good hips will not generally in my experience

Line breeding		
PARENTS	*GRANDPARENTS*	*GREAT GRANDPARENTS*
		SIRE Ch Gamegards Bulli v.d. Waldachquelle
	SIRE The Fuhrer from Gamegards	DAM Wandrin Shadow of Whitebeck
SIRE Gamegards the Protector	DAM Gamegards Roman Road	SIRE Rohirrim Seiglinde
		DAM Gamegards the Coquette
		SIRE Ch Gamegards Bulli v.d. Waldachquelle
	SIRE The Fuhrer from Gamegards	DAM Wandrin Shadow of Whitebeck
DAM Gamegards the Witch	DAM Ch Schutz from Gamegards	SIRE Ch Gamegards Bulli v.d. Waldachquelle
		DAM Lohteyn Loyalty

Above: *This pedigree illustrates line-breeding. It is important that the dogs are HD-free and of good type and temperament.*

Left: *The author with several generations of Gamegards' Rottweilers, proving the benefits of good breeding.*

---

give bad temperament and bad hips, since you are reinforcing the genes for good qualities. Of course, you have to be sure that there are no recessive genes for bad qualities. A good thing about line breeding is that if there are recessive faults it will bring them to the fore. You will learn from it, and have greater knowledge of your bloodlines and what they reproduce.

You are doubling up on what is there – good and bad – so know

the dogs in the line intimately, their faults and virtues. Some character faults to avoid in this method of breeding are hyperactivity, over-sensitivity to touch or sound, over-aggression, nervousness, biting, dullness or sluggishness. Only line breed to sterling characters which are sound mentally and physically. If you are not sure, do not do it.

Inbreeding is very close mating, ie brother to sister, father to daughter, etc. It is not a practice I use since you can make terrible mistakes if you do not know what the dogs carry genetically; you also tend to lose hybrid vigour if you do not expand your gene pool. Though some great champions in other breeds have been bred in this fashion with no ill effects, I think line breeding is a much safer procedure.

Chapter Seven

SHOWING AND COMPETITIVE TRAINING

The Breed Standards
Showing
Obedience shows

THE ROTTWEILER BREED STANDARDS

Below are both the British and American Rottweiler Breed Standards. Study them well if you want to learn about the breed.

ROTTWEILER BRITISH STANDARD

GENERAL APPEARANCE: Above average size, stalwart, dog. Correctly proportioned, compact and powerful form, permitting great strength, manoeuvrability and endurance.

CHARACTERISTICS: Appearance displays boldness and courage. Self assured and fearless. Calm gaze should indicate good humour.

TEMPERAMENT: Good natured, not nervous, aggressive or vicious; courageous, biddable, with natural guarding instincts.

HEAD AND SKULL: Head medium length, skull broad between ears. Forehead moderately arched as seen from side. Occipital bone well developed but not conspicuous. Cheeks well boned and muscled but not prominent. Skin on head not loose, although it may form a moderate wrinkle when attentive. Muzzle fairly deep with top line level, and length of muzzle in relation to distance from well-defined stop, to be as 2:3. Nose well developed with proportionately large nostrils, always black.

EYES: Medium size, almond-shaped, dark brown in colour, light eye undesirable, eyelids close-fitting.

MOUTH: Teeth strong, complete dentition with scissor bite, ie upper teeth closely overlapping the lower teeth and set square to the jaws. Flews (the fleshy upper lips) black and firm, falling gradually away towards corners of mouth, which do not protrude excessively.

EARS: Pendant, small in proportion rather than large, set high and wide apart, lying flat and close to neck.

NECK: Of fair length, strong, round and very muscular. Slightly arched, free from throatiness.

FOREQUARTERS: Shoulders well laid back, long and sloping, elbows well let down, but not loose. Legs straight, muscular, with plenty of bone and substance. Pasterns sloping slightly forward.

Above right: *A stylized diagram of a male Rottweiler showing the points of conformation together with their names.*

Below right: *The Rottweiler, as a working dog, has a skeleton built for strength and stamina. Note particularly the sturdy legs, solid shoulder and roomy chest.*

Skeleton	Conformation points
1 Skull	A Skull
2 Occiput	B Withers
3 Cervical vertebrae	C Loin
4 Scapula	D Rump
5 Thoracic vertebrae	E Stifle
6 Lumbar vertebrae	F Hock
7 Pelvis	G Underline
8 Femur	H Forearm
9 Fibula	I Pastern
10 Tibia	J Digits
11 Tarsus	K Shoulder
12 Metatarsus	L Cheek
13 Phalanges	M Flews
14 Ribs	N Underjaw
15 Ulna	O Muzzle
16 Radius	P Stop
17 Carpus	
18 Metacarpus	
19 Humerus	
20 Mandible	

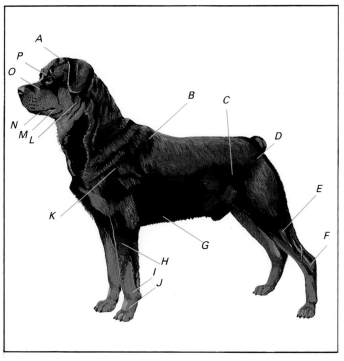

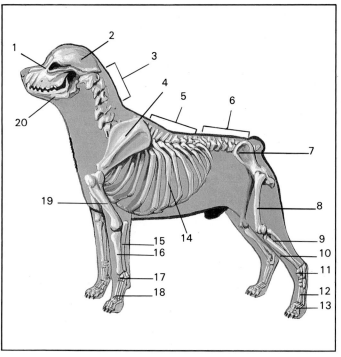

BODY: Chest roomy, broad and deep with well-sprung ribs. Depth of brisket will be not more, and not much less, than 50 per cent of shoulder height. Back straight, strong and not too long, ratio of shoulder height to length of body should be 9:10, loins short, strong and deep, flanks not tucked up. Croup of proportionate length, and broad, very slightly sloping.

HINDQUARTERS: Upper thigh broad, strongly muscled and not too short. Lower thigh well-muscled at top, strong and sinewy below. Stifles fairly well bent. Hocks well angulated without exaggeration, metatarsals not completely vertical. Strength and soundness of hock highly desirable.

FEET: Strong, round and compact with toes well arched. Hind feet somewhat longer than front. Pads very hard, toenails short, dark and strong. Rear dewclaws removed.

TAIL: Normally carried horizontally, but slightly above horizontal when dog is alert. Customarily docked at first joint, it is strong and not set too low.

GAIT/MOVEMENT: Conveys an impression of supple strength, endurance and purpose. While back remains firm and stable there is a powerful hindthrust and good stride. First and foremost, movement should be harmonious, positive and unrestricted.

COAT: Double top coat is of medium length, coarse and flat. Undercoat, essential on the neck and thighs, should not show through top coat. Hair may be a little longer on the back of the forelegs and breechings (back of the upper thigh). Long or excessively wavy coat highly undesirable.

COLOUR: Black with clearly

Above: *The head should be of medium length with a broad skull and a slightly arching forehead.*

defined markings as follows: a spot over each eye, on cheeks, as a strip around each side of muzzle (but not on bridge of nose), on throat, two clear triangles on either side of the breast bone, on forelegs from carpus downward to toes, on inside of rear legs from hock to toes (but not completely eliminating black of legs), under tail. Colour or markings from rich tan to mahogany; they should not exceed 10 per cent of body colour. White marking is highly undesirable. Black pencil markings on toes is desirable. Undercoat is grey, fawn, or black.

SIZE: Dog's height at shoulder between 25–27in (63–69cm) Bitches between 23–25in (58–63.5cm). Height should always be considered in relation to general appearance.

FAULTS: Any departure from the foregoing points should be considered a fault and the seriousness with which the fault should be regarded should be in exact proportion to its degree.

NOTE: Male animals should have two apparently normal testicles fully descended into the scrotum.

ROTTWEILER
AMERICAN STANDARD

GENERAL APPEARANCE: The ideal Rottweiler is a large, robust and powerful dog, black with clearly defined rust markings. His compact build denotes great strength, agility and endurance. Males are characteristically larger, heavier boned and more masculine in appearance.

Below: *The American Standard demands a build capable of strength and agility.*

SIZE: Males 24–27in (61–69cm) Females 22–25in (56–63.5cm) Proportion should always be considered rather than height alone. The length of the body, from breast bone (sternum) to rear edge of pelvis (ischium), is slightly longer than the height of the dog at the withers; the most desirable proportion being 10:9. Depth of chest should be 50 per cent of height. Serious faults: lack of proportion, undersize, oversize.

HEAD: Of medium length, broad between ears; forehead line seen

in profile is moderately arched. Cheekbones and stop well developed; length of muzzle should not exceed distance between stop and occiput. Skull is preferred dry; however, some wrinkling may occur when dog is alert.

MUZZLE: Bridge is straight, broad at base with slight tapering towards tip. Nose is broad rather than round, with black nostrils.

LIPS: Always black; corners tightly closed. Inner mouth pigment is dark. A pink mouth is to be penalized.

TEETH: Forty-two in number (20

Above: *The bridge of the muzzle should be straight; the nose should be broad and black.*

upper and 22 lower); strong, correctly placed, meeting in a scissors bite – lower incisors touching inside of upper incisors. Serious faults: any missing tooth, level bite. Disqualifications: undershot, overshot, four or more missing teeth.

EYES: Of medium size, moderately deep-set, almond-shaped, with well-fitting lids. Iris of uniform colour, from medium to dark brown, the darker shade

Above: *The eyes should be medium in size, dark brown in colour and almond-shaped, with well-fitting lids.*

always preferred. Serious faults: yellow (bird of prey) eyes, eyes not of same colour, eyes unequal in size or shape, hairless lid.

EARS: Pendant, proportionately small, triangular in shape; set well apart and placed on skull so as to make it appear broader when the dog is alert. Ear terminates at approximately mid cheek level. Correctly held, the inner edge will lie tightly against cheek.

NECK: Powerful, well muscled, moderately long with slight arch and without loose skin.

BODY: Topline is firm and level, extending in straight line from withers to croup. Brisket deep, reaching to elbow, chest roomy, broad with well pronounced forechest. Ribs should be well-sprung. Loin short, deep and well muscled. Croup broad, medium length, slightly sloping.

TAIL: Normally carried in horizontal position, giving impression of an elongation of top line. Carried slightly above horizontal when dog is excited. Some dogs are born without a tail, or with a very short stub. Tail is normally docked short close to the body. The set of the tail is more important than length.

FOREQUARTERS: Shoulder blade long, well laid back at 45° angle. Elbows tight, well under

body. Distance from withers to elbow and elbow to ground is equal. Legs strongly developed

Below: The upper thigh should be broad and well-muscled; look for a strong hock and thigh.

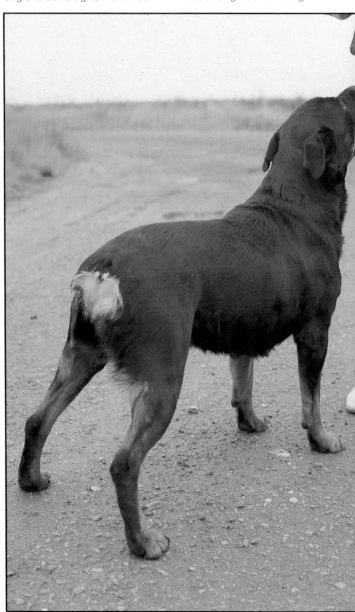

with straight heavy bone, not set closely together. Pasterns strong, springy and almost perpendicular to ground. Feet round, compact, well-arched toes, turning neither in nor out. Pads thick and hard; nails short, strong and black. Dewclaws may be removed.

HINDQUARTERS: Angulation of hindquarters balances that of forequarters. Upper thigh fairly long, broad and well muscled. Stifle joint moderately angulated. Lower thigh long, powerful, extensively muscled, leading into a strong hock joint; metatarsus nearly perpendicular to ground. Viewed from rear, hind legs are straight and wide enough apart to fit in with a properly built body. Feet somewhat longer than front feet, well-arched toes turning neither in nor out. Dewclaws must be removed if present.

COAT: Outer coat is straight, coarse, dense, medium length, lying flat. Undercoat must be present on neck and thighs, but should not show through the outer coat. The Rottweiler should be exhibited in a natural condition without trimming, except to remove whiskers, if desired. Fault: wavy coat. Serious faults: excessively short coat, curly or open coat; lack of undercoat. Disqualification: long coat.

COLOUR: Always black with rust to mahogany markings. The borderline between black and rust should be clearly defined. The markings should be located as follows: a spot over each eye; on cheeks, as a strip around each side of the muzzle, but not on the bridge of nose; on throat; triangular mark on either side of breastbone; on forelegs from carpus downward to toes; on inside of rear legs showing down the front of stifle and broadening out to front of rear legs from hock to toes, but not completely

eliminating black from back of legs; under tail. Black pencil markings on toes. The undercoat is grey or black. Quantity and location of rust markings is important and should not exceed 10 per cent of body colour. Insufficient or excessive markings should be penalized. Serious faults: excessive markings; white markings any place on dog (a few white hairs do not constitute a marking); light coloured markings. Disqualification: any base colour other than black; total absence of markings.

GAIT: The Rottweiler is a trotter. The motion is harmonious, sure, powerful and unhindered, with a strong fore-reach and a powerful rear drive. Front and rear legs are thrown neither in nor out, as the imprint of hind feet should touch that of forefeet. In a trot, the forequarters and hindquarters are mutually co-ordinated while the back remains firm; as speed is increased, legs will converge under body towards a centre line.

CHARACTER: The Rottweiler should possess a fearless expression with a self-assured aloofness that does not lend itself to immediate and indiscriminate friendships. He has an inherent desire to protect home and family, and is an intelligent dog of extreme hardness and adaptability with a strong willingness to work. A judge shall dismiss from the ring any shy or vicious Rottweiler. Shyness: a dog shall be judged fundamentally shy if, refusing to stand for examination, it shrinks away from the judge; if it fears an approach from the rear; if it shies at sudden or unusual noises to a marked degree. Viciousness: a dog that attacks or attempts to attack either the judge or its handler is definitely vicious. An aggressive or belligerent attitude towards other dogs shall not be deemed viciousness.

SHOWING

The history books tell us that the Rottweiler was first shown in competition in 1882 in Heilbronn in Germany. On that day only one dog entered, though history doesn't tell us how well it did. Things, however, have changed a great deal since then, and often not for the better.

Due to the population explosion of this breed there seem to be some people judging Rottweilers who are very inexperienced. This is a problem which one hopes will be overcome in time, when they gain the knowledge required. Sadly, many new judges think that after owning Rottweilers for a few years they are experts, whereas it is only by keeping an open mind and continuing to learn over many years that one becomes an expert – and even experts, if wise, never stop learning. Beware the instant expert judges, the judges who are rough or over-handle the dogs, and the judges who have so little confidence in their own judgement that they put up only well-known, or their friends', dogs.

How do you select your shows and judges? I am afraid that it is by trial and error; by attending shows under a variety of judges you will soon learn which ones to avoid. Shows are advertised in weekly or monthly dog magazines with the address and telephone number of the Show Secretary. If you contact them, they will send you a schedule with an entry form.

Having filled in your entry form and posted it off before the closing date, with the correct fee, you then put in a little extra show training. Daily sessions of about 5–10 minutes, teaching your dog to stand in a natural but flattering position, trot on a loose lead, and ignore other dogs, should have already taken place by the time you enter your first show. At the

moment there is a silly fashion in Britain for the handler to stand in front of the dog with the handler's knee almost touching the dog's breastbone. This causes the dog to gaze up with the nose pointing skywards, masking the dog's front and spoiling the profile of the dog. Judges need to see the dog standing in a natural way with the head looking forward, not upward, showing off the lay of the shoulder and crest of the

Below: *In the show ring, ignoring other dogs is as important as performing a correct trot.*

Bottom: *A perfect show position should show off the front part of the dog: the lay of the shoulder and the neck.*

neck. The front of the dog should be clearly visible and a good handler should be almost invisible.

Teach your dog to walk into the 'stand' position on a loose lead, tell it to 'stay' and move back; you may use a titbit, but keep your hands down so that the dog is not looking up all the time.

Get various friends to 'go over' the dog for you, gently feeling the back, thighs and shoulders. If the dog gets upset upon examination, then go back to your 'stand stay' training and teach the dog to 'stand stay' no matter who touches it. It is wise to show the judge the dog's teeth yourself and if you have done your homework in teaching the dog to stand, and let you peel back the lips to expose the teeth, all will be well.

If your dog has heavy feathering on the hind legs and the tail has a few longish hairs, it is permissible to clip the long hair neatly so that the dog looks more clean cut.

Get to the show in good time so that your dog has a chance to settle in and go to the 'dog loo' area.

When you get into the ring, relax and enjoy it. Concentrate on displaying your dog to the best advantage; if you are placed, it is a nice bonus, but most of all, enjoy your day and be sure that your dog does too.

Do not leave your dog unattended on the bench, as

——— Show tips ———
Remember on show day to take:
(a) Collar, benching chain, water and bowl
(b) Ring card clips (you can buy these at most shows)
(c) Titbits (some people use a belt with a titbit bag on it)
(d) Brush, chamois leather
(e) Blanket for the bench (if it is a benched show)
(f) Exhibitor's passes

---

there have been dogs stolen or interfered with at some shows. Weirdos lurk everywhere and some show-goers become very nasty and spiteful if you win and they don't. Whatever happens, try to be a nice exhibitor and not one of the loud-mouthed varieties; be kind to others and don't crow if you win. Take a win or a beating with the same good grace. After all, it is the dog you love going home with you, be it a winner or a loser and who knows, things could be reversed next time out. If you want to leave your dog on the bench and look around the show, it is a good idea to make friends with another exhibitor and let them watch your dog, then you can offer to watch theirs in return.

Below: *Show benches can be made more comfortable with a blanket and water bowl.*

Never leave dogs in cars at shows – this has caused death on just moderately warm days. Do not chance it, as it is a horrible way for a dog to die. In America I have seen Rottweilers wearing wet towelling dog coats to keep them cool at shows on hot days. It is a good idea, since this breed is not at its best in extremely hot weather.

Working Trials are more difficult, but I find them much more enjoyable. The work is harder and more practical, there is less emphasis on precision and more on real working ability. CD (Companion Dog) class is:
1. Heel on lead
2. Heel free
3. Send away
4. Recall
5. Retrieve a dumbbell on the flat
6. Scale jump 6ft (1.8m)
7. Clear jump 3ft (0.9m)
8. Long jump 9ft (2.7m)
9. Sit Stay 2 minutes, handler out of sight
10. Down Stay 10 minutes, handler out of sight
11. Search an area of 15sq yd (12sq m) for four scented articles. You are allowed only four minutes for this exercise.

You must obtain half marks in each exercise to qualify, and this is what you are working towards, not necessarily to winning

In America, to qualify for the Companion Dog (CD) (Novice) class, the dog must score 170–200 points at three different American Kennel Club (AKC) shows. The dog must:
1. Heel on leash
2. Heel off leash
3. Stand for examination
4. Come on command
5. One minute sit stay
6. Three minute down stay

In my teens I did Working Trials with a red/white English Bull Terrier bitch and when she retired at eight years old I was sure I would never find another Bull Terrier which could jump like her. Having had Bull Terriers since childhood I could not find another breed I really wanted until I saw my first Rottweiler working – Mrs Mcphail's Rintelna the Bombadier CDEX UDEX. It was love at first sight and I was

Below: *Showing off how well a Rottweiler can work: taking the clear jump with lots to spare.*

Above: *A safer test of ability than the scale jump: an 'A' frame avoids a risky high drop.*

soon the proud owner of his son, Emil from Blackforest (Panzer). He was the best dog I have ever owned. As well as working and qualifying at trials, he did over 900 film and television parts.

Trialling is a rewarding pastime, but there is one big snag in Britain at the moment: the scale jump. It is very hard on a Rottweiler's shoulders, as coming down from 6ft (1.8m) is jarring and can cause serious injury. There are groups of people lobbying for an A frame at trials, as it is just as testing of agility and allows more breeds, such as Springer Spaniels, Bull Terriers and other, shorter-legged heavy dogs, to compete. Trials should be for everyone, not just the working breeds.

For the UD (Utility Dog) stake the dogs must do all the CD work, plus track a scent, and for each stake – WD (Working Dog), TD (Tracker Dog), up to PD (Police Dog) – the work becomes progressively more difficult. PD includes attack work as well, and even greater control exercises like recall from a fleeing criminal without biting, searching for a hidden person and speaking but not biting are taught. Those dogs which qualify PDEX have really been trained well and are totally under control.

For the show ring your dog must be clean and shining, fit not fat, and completely well-behaved at all times.

Showing is becoming a very serious business nowadays, and the days when I got tied to a tent post at Windsor Championship Show just before the Open Bitch Class for a joke are long gone. I was untied just in time to dash into the ring and win a first prize with my old Champion Schutz!

OBEDIENCE SHOWS

The rules of competitive obedience shows and trials vary from country to country, but let me tell you what a dog needs to do in Britain in, for example, Novice Obedience.
1. Heel on lead
2. Heel free
3. Retrieve a dumbbell on the flat
4. Recall to handler
5. Sit Stay 1 minute
6. Down Stay 3 minutes
7. Stand Stay
8. Temperament test on lead

The standard is very high, with the fast, super-attentive Border Collies being very hard to beat. You need great precision in obedience in order to win, and must practise very hard under expert guidance. Join the best dog obedience class you can find, making sure that the instructors really know their job. Some instructors go off on a month's course and come back with a piece of paper which says 'You are now a dog trainer'. That's fine, but you should establish that they really do have practical experience. What have they won? Have they worked any other dog than a Border Collie or German Shepherd? Watch them carefully with their own dogs: are the animals happy, willing workers? Can the instructor tell you in simple terms what you need to know?

If you get a good instructor and attend a good club he or she will soon point out your faults and help you to achieve better results. There is not enough space here for a full guide on

Top: *The chase begins. Attack work requires total obedience and strict training. It should never be taught unnecessarily.*

Right: *The man has failed to outrun the dog, and the dog strikes. Note the leather protection on the man's arm.*

Top: *The dog will hold the 'criminal' until given the release command by the handler.*

competitive training – it needs a book all to itself, so I have included a list of titles at the back of this book.

I am against members of the general public teaching their dogs to attack, as you need to have incredible obedience and control before you do this and very few people can be bothered to do all the hard work of the control exercises. Some people are eager to have a Rottweiler which attacks but do not have the discipline to put into it, and this can be highly dangerous. I will give you an example of the sort of thing which happened to me with my 'Panzer'.

I was meeting my ex-husband; he came out of a doorway in a crowd of people when the dog and I were some distance away and I told 'Panzer' to go and meet him, letting the dog off the leash to go. Just at that moment a man came out of the crowd and began to run fast, away from us. Panzer, who was attack trained, made a misjudgement and misinterpreted my command. As the dog went into top gear I realized what had happened and

yelled 'Down Panzer!' Fortunately we had done our control exercises and the dog dropped down about three paces from the running man who, incidentally, was totally unaware that behind him was a Rottweiler intent on grabbing him. The man went on his way and I recalled the dog, but just imagine what could have happened had the dog not been obedient. Such incidents can occur with an attack trained dog, so you see why the control is so important.

The Rottweiler can bite much harder than, say, a German Shepherd or a Doberman and can inflict terrible damage. I have seen the scars of such bites and they are not a pretty sight, so please do not encourage an untrained Rottweiler to bite anyone. Your Rottweiler has an inbuilt guarding instinct and, when mature, will protect you well, although just the fact that you have a Rottweiler by your side will deter most wrongdoers.

I hope that you will do some training work with your dog, since it is one of the most rewarding pastimes and pays dividends in everyday life. You need only some spare time, a dog, and a little know how to have a whole new set of experiences opened up for you.

Appendix I

Glossary of dog terminology

Almond eyes: Oval-shaped like an almond, slanted at corners.

Angulation: Angle created by two joining bones; particularly, the shoulder and hock.

Bad mouth: Teeth crooked or misaligned overshot or undershot bite.

Barrel hocks: Turned-out hocks, (also called spread hocks, or divergent hocks).

Bench show: A show at which the dogs are 'benched' (leashed on benches).

Best in Show: The animal judged to be the best of all the breeds in a show.

Bitch: A female dog.

Bite: The position of the teeth when the mouth is shut.

Blanket: The coat colour on the back and upper part of the sides.

Blooded: Of good breeding; pedigreed.

Board: To kennel and care for a dog in its owner's absence, for a fee.

Bobtail: A tailless dog, or a dog with a very short docked tail.

Bodied up: Well-developed.

Bone: A well-boned dog is one with limbs that give an appearance and feel of strength and spring without coarseness.

Bossy: With over-development of the shoulder muscles.

Brace: A pair of dogs of the same type.

Breastbone: Bone running down the middle of the chest, to which all but the floating ribs are attached.

Breed: A variety of purebred dog; a dog or bitch with a pedigree.

Breeder: Someone who breeds dogs.

Breeding particulars: Sire, dam, date of birth, sex, colour, Kennel Club registration details, etc.

Brisket: The part of the lower chest that includes the breastbone.

Brood bitch: A bitch kept for breeding.

Burr: The irregular inner part of the pinna of the ear.

Canines: The two upper and two lower pointed teeth next to the incisors.

Carpals: Pastern joint bones.

Carp back: Arched back.

Castrate: To surgically remove the testicles of a male; to geld.

Champion: A dog that has won three Challenge Certificates under three different judges at Championship shows in the UK. In the USA the title is awarded on points won at major shows.

Chest: The body enclosed by the ribs.

Choke chain: A chain or leather collar fitted to the dog's neck in such a way that the amount of pressure exerted by hand tightens or loosens it. Also referred to as a check chain.

Collar: A circle of leather or chain used to direct and control the dog when the leash (lead) is attached.

Condition: Health of the dog, shown by coat, weight, appearance and deportment.

Conformation: Form and structure, make-up and shape of a dog; the arrangement of the parts in conformance with breed standard requirements.

Cow hocked: Hocks turned towards one another.

Crossbred: The progeny of purebred parents of different breeds.

Croup: The rear part of the back above the hind legs.

Cryptorchid: An adult dog whose testicles have not descended into the scrotum. A dog of this type cannot be exhibited.

Dam: The mother of a litter of puppies.

Dew claw: A claw on the inside of the leg, which is usually removed in early puppyhood but retained by some breeds.

Diagonals: Right front and left rear legs form the right diagonal; left front and right rear legs form the left diagonal. In the trot the diagonals move together.

Disqualify: A decision made by a judge or show committee, ruling that a dog has a condition making it ineligible for further competition under the dog show rules or under the *standard* for its breed.

Distemper teeth: Teeth marked, pitted, ringed and often stained, due to distemper or other severe infection.

Dock: To shorten the tail by cutting, usually done in early puppyhood if breed standards demand.

Dog show: An exhibition at which dogs are judged in accordance with an established standard of perfection for each breed.

Drive: A solid thrusting of the hind-quarters denoting sound locomotion.

Elbow: The upper arm and forearm joint.

Entropion: A condition in which the eyelid turns inward and the lashes irritate the eyeball.

Even bite: Meeting of upper and lower front teeth at edges with no overlap.

Expression: The general appearance of the front of the head, as typical of the breed.

Eye-teeth: The upper canines.

Fancier: Someone active in the sport of breeding, showing and judging purebred dogs.

Flank: The body area between the last rib and the hip.

Flat withers: An unattractive fault that is the result of short upright shoulder blades that abruptly join the withers.

Flews: Hanging upper lips, like those of a Bulldog, usually refers to the lateral parts of the lips.

Floating rib: The last, or 13th rib, which is unattached to other ribs of the rib-cage.

Flying trot: A fast gait in which all the feet are off the ground for a brief second during each half stride. Also called suspension trot.

Forearm: The foreleg bone between the elbow and the pastern.

Foreface: The front part of the head, before the eyes; the muzzle.

Foster mother: A bitch used to nurse another animal's whelps.

Front: The whole front part of the body.

Gait: A style of movement, e.g. running or trotting.

Groom: To brush, comb, trim and prepare a dog's coat for show or pleasure.

Handler: A person who handles (shows) a dog at dog shows, field trials, or obedience tests.

Haunches: Back part of the thigh on which the dog sits.

Haw: A third eyelid or nictitating membrane in the inside corner of the eye.

Heat: Seasonal period of the female, normally this occures every six months.

Heel: Command by handler to keep the dog close to his heel.

Heel free: Command whereby the dog must walk to heel without a lead.

Height: Dog's height measured from the ground to the top of the shoulder.

Hind-quarters: Rear anatomy of dog (pelvis, thighs, hocks and paws).

Hip dysplasia: Malformation of the ball of the hip joint, usually hereditary.

Hocks: Those joints in the hind limbs below the true knees, or stifle joints.

Inbreeding: Mating within the same family: a bitch to her sons, or a dog to his daughters.

Incisors: The upper and lower front teeth, between the canines.

In season: In heat ready for mating.

Ischium: Hip bone.

Kiss marks: Tan spots on the coat on the cheeks and over the eyes.

Lead: A strap cord or chain attached to the collar or harness for the purpose of restraining or leading the dog: a leash.

Level back: One that makes a straight line from withers to tail, but is not necessarily parallel to the ground.

Level bite: When the front teeth incisors of the upper and lower jaws meet edge to edge.

Licence: Permission granted by the AKC to a non-member club to hold a dog show, or obedience test for field trial. In the UK, all shows in which purebred dogs are exhibited are held under Kennel Club licence.

Line breeding: The mating of related dogs of the same breed, within the line, or family, to a common ancestor, e.g. a dog to his grand-dam.

Loin: The part of the body between the last rib and the back legs.

Match show: An informal dog show at which no Championship points are awarded.

Mate: The breeding of dog and bitch.

Milk teeth: First teeth. (Puppies lose these at 4–6 months.)

Molars: Dogs have two molars on each side of the upper jaw, and three on each side of the lower jaw. Upper molars have three roots, lower have two roots.

Muzzle: The part of the head containing the mouth and nose. A device to prevent biting.

Neck well set on: Good neckline, merging with strong withers, forming a transition into topline.

Occiput: Upper, back point of the skull

Overhang: A heavy or pronounced brow.

Over-reaching: Fault in the trot caused by more angulation and drive from behind than in front, so that the rear feet are forced to step to one side of the forefeet to avoid touching.

Overshot: When the upper teeth project beyond the lower; also called pig jaw.

Pads: The tough, cushioned soles of the feet.

Paper foot: A flat foot with thin pads.

Pastern: The region of the foreleg between the carpus (wrist) and the digits.

Peak: A prominent occiput.

Pedigree: Written record of the names of a dog's ancestors going back at least three generations.

Pencilling: The dark lines on the surface of the toes in some breeds, notably the English Toy Terrier [Manchester Terrier (Toy)].

Points: Colour correlated on face, ears, legs and tail – usually white, black or tan.

Puppy: A dog under one year old.

Purebred: A dog whose sire and dam belong to the same breed and are themselves of unmixed descent since the recognition of the breed.

Reach of front: Length of forward stride taken by forelegs without wasted or excessive motion.

Register: To record details of a dog's breeding with the respective Kennel Club.

Scapula: The shoulder blade.

Scissor bite: A bite in which the upper front teeth slightly overlap the lower front teeth.

Sire: The father of a litter puppies.

Smooth coat: Short, sleek hair lying close to the skin.

Soundness: The state of mental and physical health when all organs and faculties are functioning normally.

Spay: The surgical removal (hysterectomy) of the bitch's reproductive organs to stop conception.

Speak: To bark.

Splay feet: Feet with toes spread wide.

Spring of ribs: Curvature of ribs for heart and lung capacity.

Stance: Manner of standing.

Standard: The standard of perfection for each breed.

Stifle: That joint in the hind leg of a dog approximating to the knee in man, particularly relating to the inner side.

Stop: The depression between and in front of the eyes, roughly corresponding to the bridge of the nose.

Straight hocks: Hocks that are absolutely straight vertically.

Stud: Male used for breeding.

Stud book: A record of the breeding particulars of recognized breeds.

Topline: The outline of the dog from behind the withers to the tail set.

Trot: A two-beat diagonal gait in which the feet at diagonally opposite ends of the body strike the ground together: right hind with left front and left hind with right front.

Type: The characteristic qualities distinguishing a breed, the embodiment of a standard.

Undershot: Having the lower jaw protecting the opposite of *overshot*.

Upper arm: The humerus or foreleg bone between the shoulder blade and the forearm.

Vent: Both the anal opening and the small area of light hair directly beneath the tail.

Whelping: Giving birth to puppies.

Whelps: Newly born puppies.

Withers: The highest point of the shoulders, just behind the neck.

Wry mouth: Mouth in which the lower jaw does not line up with the upper.

Appendix II

Abbreviations

A.D.R.K.	Allgemeiner Deutscher Rottweiler Klub – General German Rottweiler Club
AI	Artificial Insemination
AKC	American Kennel Club
ANKC	Australian National Kennel Club
AOC	Any other colour
AVNSC	Any Variety Not Separately Classified
B	Bitch
BIS	Best in Show
BOB	Best of Breed
BOS	Best Opposite Sex
CAC	Certificat d'apitude au Championnat de Beauté
CACIB	Certificat d'apitude au Championnat International de Beauté
CC	Challenge Certificate
CD	Companion Dog
CDEX	Companion Dog Excellent
Ch	Champion
CKC	Canadian Kennel Club
D	Dog
FCI	Federation Cynologique Internationale
Int Ch	International Champion
JW	Junior Warrant
KC	Kennel Club (UK)
LKA	Ladies Kennel Association
LOF	Livre des Origines Francais (French Stud Book)
LOSH	Livre Origines St Hubert (Belgian Stud Book)
NAF	Name applied for
Nordic Ch	Nordic Champion
OBCh	Obedience Champion
P	Puppy
PD	Police Dog
PV	Parvo virus
TD	Tracker Dog
UD	Utility Dog
UDEX	Utility Dog Excellent
WD	Working Dog

Useful Addresses

Kennel Clubs
Australia Australian National Kennel Council, Royal Show Grounds, Ascot Vale, Victoria
Belgium Societe Royale Saint-Hubert, Avenue de l'Armee 25, B-1040, Brussels
Canada Canadian Kennel Club, 2150 Bloor Street West, Toronto M6S 1M8, Ontario
France Societe Centrale Canine, 215 Rue St Denis, 75083 Paris, Cedex O2
Germany Verband ffur das Deutsche Hundewesen (VDH), Postfach 1390, 46 Dortmund
Holland Raad van Beheer op Kynologisch Gebied in Nederland, Emmalaan 16, Amsterdam, Z
Ireland Irish Kennel Club, 23 Earlsfort Terrace, Dublin 2
Italy Ente Nazionale Della Cinofilia Italiana, Viale Premuda, 21 Milan
New Zealand New Zealand Kennel Club, Private Bag, Porirua, New Zealand
Spain Real Sociedad Central de Fomento de las razas en Espana, Los Madrazo 20, Madrid 14
United Kingdom The Kennel Club, 1-4 Clarges Street, London W1Y 8AB
United States of America American Kennel Club, 51 Madison Avenue, New York, NY 10010: The United Kennel Club Inc, 100 East Kilgore Road, Kalamazoo, MI 49001-5598

General Addresses
The United Kingdom
The Agility Club The Spinney, Aubrey Lane, Redbourn, Hertfordshire AL3 7AN
British Small Animals Veterinary Association 7 Mansfield Street, London W1M 0AT
British Veterinary Association 7 Mansfield Street, London W1M 0AT
National Canine Defence League 1 Pratt Mews, London NW1 0AD
The Royal Society for the Prevention of Cruelty to Animals RSPCA Headquarters, Causeway, Horsham, Sussex RH12 1HG

The United States
American Animal Hospital Association 3612 East Jefferson, South Bend, Indiana 46615
American Society for the Prevention of Cruelty to Animals 441 East 92nd Street, New York 10028
American Veterinary Medical Association 930 North Meacham Road, Schaumburg, Illinois 60196
Orthopaedic Foundation for Animals 817 Virginia Avenue, Columbia, Missouri 65201

Rottweiler Clubs
Some Breed Clubs in Britain
The Rottweiler Club, Sec: Mrs M Hembrow, 21 Palmyra Road, Elson, Gosport, Hants PO12 4EE
British Rottweiler Assoc. Midland Rottweiler Club, Northern Rottweiler Club, Scottish Rottweiler Club, Welsh Rottweiler Club and Northern Ireland Rottweiler Club.
  Addresses of secretaries of the above clubs can be obtained from the Kennel Club, 1-4 Clarges Street, London W1Y 8AB
Some Breed Clubs in America
American Rottweiler Club, Sec.; Ms Doreen LePage, 960 South Main St, Pascoag, RI 02859.
Colonial Rottweiler Club (Philadelphia), Medallion Rottweiler Club (Chicago), Golden State Rottweiler Club (Los Angeles), Western Rottweiler Owners (California), Houston Bay Area Rottweiler Club (Texas), Texas Rottweiler Club, Orange Coast Rottweiler Club (California), Tidewater Rottweiler Club (Virginia). Addresses of secretaries of the above clubs can be obained from the American Kennel Club, 51 Madison Avenue, New York, NY 10010

Other Rottweiler Clubs
Australia: Rottweiler Club of Victoria, Rottweiler Club of South Australia
Canada: The Rottweiler Club of Canada
New Zealand: Central Rottweiler Club Inc

Further Reading
Breed Books
The Complete Rottweiler, Muriel, Freeman, Howell Book House, USA
All About the Rottweiler, Mary Macphail, Pelham Books, London
The Rottweiler, Midland Rottweiler Club, UK
The Rottweiler, Dr Dogmar Hodinar, Von Palisaden Publications, USA
Training
Training Your Dog, the step-by-step manual. Volhard & Fisher, Howell Book House, USA
The Agility Dog, Peter Lewis, Canine Publications, UK
Training Your Dog, Joan Palmer, Salamander Books Ltd, London 1986
General
Practical Dog Breeding and Genetics, Eleanor Frankling, Popular Dogs, London
The Conformation of the Dog, R H Smyth, Popular Dogs, London
Canine Terminology, H Spira, Harper & Row, Sydney

Above: *Properly socialized and well-trained, your Rottweiler should be a companion to be cherished.*

Understanding Your Dog, Michael W Fox, The Anchor Press Ltd, UK
Dog Steps, R P Elliot, Howell Book House, New York
All About Your Dog's Health, GP West, Pelham Books, London
Understanding Your Dog, PR Messent, Quarto Publishing, London
First Aid For Pet Animals, BM Bush, A&C Black, UK.

Magazines
The United Kingdom
The Kennel Gazette, 1-5 Clarges Street, Piccadilly, London W1Y 8AB.
Dog World, 9 Tufton Street, Ashford, Kent TN23 1QN.
Our Dogs, Oxford Road, Station Approach, Manchester.
Dogs Monthly, Unit One, Bowen Industrial Estate, Aberbargoed, Bargoed, Mid-Glamorgan, CF8 9ET.

The United States
Dog World Magazine, 300 West Adams Street, Chicago, Il 60606.
Pure-Bred Dogs/American Kennel Gazette, 51 Madison Avenue, New York, NY 10010.